Sep 2007

Happy Birthday
Cameron!!

Loads g love

Auntie Fran.

JUNIOR
NATURE GUIDE
BIRDS

Written by Angela Royston

www.alligatorbooks.co.uk

Bird-watcher's Code

1 Always go bird-watching with a friend, and always tell an adult where you are going.

2 Observe and photograph birds without disturbing them.

3 Don't touch or pick up fledglings and eggs. If you do, the parents may abandon them and they will die.

4 Ask permission before exploring or crossing private property.

5 Keep a good distance from nests and nesting colonies and leave birds in peace.

6 Keep to existing roads, tracks and paths wherever possible.

7 Leave all gates as you find them.

8 Take your litter home.

© 2007 Alligator Books Limited
Published by Alligator Books Limited
Gadd House, Arcadia Avenue,
London N3 2JU

Printed in Malaysia

Contents

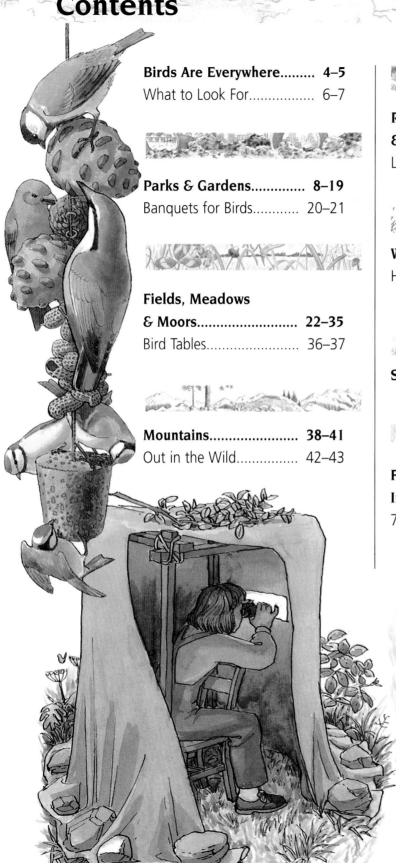

Birds are Everywhere

About 600 different types of birds breed in Great Britain and Europe, but many other kinds – over 200 species – visit here as well. If you are not an expert bird-watcher, trying to identify one bird among so many can be hard to do.

If you really want to get to know birds and where to see them, you have to be a naturalist, not just a bird-watcher. Birds rely on their surroundings for food, places to roost (sleep) and good nesting sites, and these vary from habitat to habitat. When you know what a habitat provides, you will know which birds you might expect to see there.

This book will make this job easier for you in two ways. It shows you only the birds you are most likely to see, and it puts them in groups according to the habitat, or kind of countryside, where you are most likely to see them.

So, don't look for a Puffin in a forest or a Red Grouse by the sea. They know where they are most likely to find the food they eat and, with practice, so will you.

From egg to bird

If you watch birds regularly you will see birds at all stages of their lives. But don't expect any particular bird always to look just like the picture in this book. Its colour and markings may be different if it is a female or a young bird. Males are usually the most brightly coloured. Their markings show best during the breeding season when they are trying to attract the females.

A new brood of birds are growing inside these eggs.

Young birds are called fledglings. Their fluffy feathers are often brown to camouflage them from other birds and animals that might eat them.

Once the fledglings can fly, they have to feed themselves.

When birds are fully grown, they find a mate, build a nest, and start to raise a brood of young.

How to use this book

To identify a bird that you don't recognize, such as the hawk and the sparrow shown here, follow these steps. (Throughout this guide, bird 'size' is measured from beak tip to tail tip.)

1 **Draw a field sketch** quickly as shown on page 43. First make sure of its size and shape. Then look for any special features (pages 6–7 show you the kind of things you should look for).

2 **Decide what habitat you are in.** If you are not sure, read the descriptions at the start of each section to see which one fits best. Each habitat has a different picture band heading and these are shown below.

3 **Look through the pages of birds** with this picture band. The picture and information for each bird will help you to identify it. The large bird (above left) is a Hen Harrier (see page 25 to find out more).

4 **If you can't find the bird there**, look through the other sections. Birds move around and you will surely see many of them in more than one habitat. You will find the small bird (below left) is a House Sparrow (see page 16).

5 **If you still can't find the bird**, you may have to look in a larger field guide (see page 78 for some suggestions). You may have spotted a very rare bird!

Top-of-page Picture Bands

This book is divided into different habitats. Each habitat (type of countryside) has a different picture band at the top of the page. These are shown below.

Parks & Gardens

Fields, Meadows & Moors

Mountains

Rivers, Lakes & Marshes

Woodlands

Seashores

What To Look For

Parts of a bird

When you are trying to identify a bird, look for patches of colour and stripes on its wings, tail and body. Is the colour of its back different from its chest or belly? Does it have eye stripes or chin stripes? In this book, the description of each bird tells you the colours and markings you are most likely to see.

Wing bar

Crown

Forehead

Nape

Eye stripe

Back

Cheek

Chin

Neck

Flight feathers

Breast

Belly

Rump

Tail bar

Outer tail feathers

Bills or beaks

The shape of a bird's bill depends on the kind of food that it eats.

A wader has a long, thin bill for catching small animals.

A heron is a wading bird. It uses its very long bill to stab fish in shallow water.

A hawk has a sharp, hooked bill for tearing meat.

A duck has a flat bill for dabbling in water to sift for tiny creatures.

A finch has a short, stout bill for cracking seeds.

Wing shapes

When a bird is flying, look at the shape of its wings and the pattern of its flight.

A finch has short, broad wings for flitting from tree to tree.

A swift has narrow, swept-back wings for flying fast through the air.

An eagle has long, broad wings for soaring and hovering.

A seagull has straight, narrow wings for soaring and gliding over the sea.

Feet and legs

The shape of a bird's feet and legs tell you about the way it lives.

Hawks and other birds of prey use their sharp talons for grasping their prey.

Tree-climbers, such as woodpeckers, use their long toes and claws to grip the tree trunks.

Ground birds, such as pheasants, have strong, thick toes to scratch with.

Waterbirds, such as ducks, have webbed feet for paddling through water.

Parks & Gardens

You may think your garden is too small to be of much interest to birds, but, along with all the other gardens nearby, it provides a rich source of food and shelter for them. They can roost at night in thick bushes and trees. In spring, watch for them nesting there too.

Thrushes and blackbirds will look for worms and snails on the lawn or for spiders and insects around the garden shed or under the shrubs. Finches and many other birds will feed on the seeds, shoots and berries of the plants themselves.

Parks are like very large gardens, but they often have the added attractions of large trees and a lake. You may see larger birds here, such as moorhens, ducks and some of the other birds that normally live on lakes and marshes. These park birds are much tamer than those that live in the countryside.

Most of the birds that come into your garden, however, are woodland birds that have learned to live in the artificial habitat of parks and gardens. Some have found gardens so good that more of them live there now than in woods. The picture shows twelve birds from this book; how many can you recognize?

Blackbird, Chaffinch, Collared Dove, Greenfinch, House Sparrow, Starling, Blue Tit, Coal Tit, Great Tit, Pied Wagtail, Wren.

Parks & Gardens

House Martin

You can tell a House Martin from a Swallow or Swift by its obvious white underparts and white rump. It flies very fast, twisting and turning in the air to catch flying insects. Its wings are almost triangular. It builds a nest of mud under the eaves of roofs or under bridges. A Swallow's nest is an open cup, but House Martins leave only a tiny entrance hole in theirs. They lay four to five eggs at a time, but may raise two or three broods a year.

Family: Swallows and Martins
Size: Up to 12 cm – Call: 'CHIRRUP' – Summer visitor

Swallow

Swallows fly much lower than Swifts, hunting for flying insects, but you can tell a Swallow from a Swift by its long, forked tail and pale underside. Look too for the red face and throat and blue back. Those with red underparts are more typical of the Eastern Mediterranean type. Swallows often fly close to the ground and over lakes and rivers where there are plenty of insects. They build a nest of mud inside barns or garages and lay four to six eggs. In autumn, large flocks of Swallows gather on telegraph wires before they migrate to southern Africa for the winter.

Family Group: Swallows and Martins
Size: Up to 19 cm
Call: Sharp 'TSWIT'. Also has a twittering song – Summer visitor

Green Woodpecker

You will probably hear the Green Woodpecker before you see it. It has a bright red head, a green back and a yellow underside, but you are most likely to notice its yellow rump as it flies away. Look for it on the ground as well as in trees. It hops clumsily about looking for ants to eat. Its droppings look like cigarette ash, but they are just the remains of hundreds of ants. Both male and female carve out the nest hole in the trunk of a tree. The female lays five to seven white eggs.

Family Group: Woodpecker
Size: Up to 32 cm
Call: Loud and laughing
Also found in woods

Jay

Jays have pinkish bodies and dark tails. When they fly, you should easily recognize the big white rump and bright blue patches on their wings. Their flight is rather jerky and you will see them on their own or in pairs. They particularly like oak woods and store acorns in autumn. They also feed on insects, fruit and seeds. In spring, they steal the eggs and young birds from other nests. Jays build a nest shaped like a cup of twigs lined with roots where they lay five or six eggs.

Family Group: Crow
Size: Up to 34 cm
Call: Harsh shrieking
Also found in woods

Swift

Swifts are perfectly suited to flying. You will often see several of them flying fast, wheeling high in the sky. They are black all over with long, narrow wings and short, forked tails. Once they leave the nest, they may not land again for months or even years. They catch flying insects, and sleep, drink and find nesting material in the air. They usually nest in the roof of a building. They build the nest with leaves and feathers which they have collected in mid-air before the female lands to lay two to three eggs. In autumn, Swifts migrate to Africa for the winter.

Family Group: Swift
Size: Up to 16 cm
Call: Shrill screaming
Summer visitor

Kestrel

Look for Kestrels hovering in the air or perched on a post. The male of this small bird of prey has a bluish grey head and tail, with a reddish brown back. When it hovers, you will see its long, pointed wings and paler underparts. Keep watching and you might see it glide down and drop onto its prey, usually a small mammal, bird, worm or insect. Kestrels usually nest on ledges of buildings or cliffs or in holes in trees, but they will also use nest-boxes. They lay three to six eggs.

Family Group: Falcon
Size: Up to 34 cm
Call: Loud 'KEE-KEE-KEE'
Also seen over moors and motorways

Parks & Gardens

Black Redstart

Black Redstarts are much rarer than Blackbirds but, if you do see a Black Redstart, you can recognize it by its red tail and much smaller size. It likes to perch on the ground or on rocks or walls. Notice how it flicks its tail all the time. It likes to build its nest of moss and grass in ruined buildings and power stations. It lays four to six eggs.

Family Group: Thrush
Size: Up to 14 cm
Call: Shrill 'TSIP'. Also a short musical snatch
Not found in Scandinavia or northern Britain

Hoopoe

Despite its striking pattern, in the strong sunshine and shade around the Mediterranean the Hoopoe is hard to spot. Its body is pinkish brown and its large, rounded wings are black and white. It spends a lot of time on the ground. Look for its long, curved bill which it uses to probe the grass for insect larvae. It also catches large insects and small lizards. It builds its nest in trees or among rocks and lays five to eight eggs.

Family group: Hoopoe
Size: Up to 28 cm
**Call: Whooping
'POOOOP-POOOOP-POOOOP'**
**Also found on open
ground with trees**
Rare in Britain and Scandinavia
Summer visitor

Collared Dove

Look out for the black band around the back of the neck of this small, pinkish grey pigeon. When it is flying, look for the dark wing feathers and long tail with a white tail band. Collared Doves like to eat grain, leaves and seeds. They build a flimsy nest of twigs in a tree or building. Although they lay only two white eggs at a time, they have up to five broods each year. In the last eighty years, they have spread quickly from Asia through most of Europe.

Family Group: Pigeons and Doves
Size: Up to 32 cm
Call: Abrupt cooing 'COO-COOOO-CUK'

Starling

Starlings have glossy black feathers which gleam with purple and oily green. In winter, they are flecked with white spots. They strut around the garden, probing the ground for insects. They often take over on bird-tables, pushing out the other birds. Starlings gather in huge, noisy flocks to roost together just before sunset. Some roosts have over a million birds in them. They nest in holes in trees and under the eaves of roofs. They lay four to six eggs in a cup of grass lined with feathers or finer grass.

Family Group: Starling
Size: Up to 21 cm
Call: Jumbled song which includes imitations of other birds
Also common near farms

Song Thrush

You can tell a Song Thrush by its brown-spotted underparts and brown upperparts. Look for the pale orange under its wing as it flies. Listen for it singing last thing before dark. It repeats first one phrase over and over again, then another. Song Thrushes feed on worms, insects and fruit but they are most famous for smashing snails against a stone, or 'anvil', to break the shells. In autumn, they eat berries. They nest in a bush or a tree and lay three to five eggs in a large cup of grass, moss and mud.

Family Group: Thrush
Size: Up to 23 cm
Call: Sharp 'TSIP'. Song is loud and repetitive
Also found in woods and fields

Blackbird

You can easily recognize a male Blackbird by its glossy black feathers and bright yellow beak (the female is dark brown). Notice how it raises its tail just after landing. You may spot it hopping across the grass in search of earthworms, or you may hear it rustling through the dead leaves looking for worms, insects and snails. Listen out for it at dawn and dusk when it perches high above the ground and sings its loud musical song. It nests in thick bushes or trees and lays three to five eggs in an untidy cup of moss, grass and mud.

Family Group: Thrush
Size: Up to 25 cm
Call: Scolding 'TUC, TUC'
Also a rich, tuneful song

Spotted Flycatcher

Chiffchaff

Chiffchaffs and Willow Warblers are almost impossible to tell apart, unless you hear their song. Both birds are greenish on top and paler underneath. Young ones look yellowy. Look for the pale stripe above the eye. The Chiffchaff's song is a series of 'chiff-chaff' notes repeated in any order. Like other warblers, Chiffchaffs feed on insects. They may catch them in the air or sometimes hover and pick them from under a leaf. Their nest is a dome of leaves and grass built in bushes such as bramble. The female lays five or six eggs.

Family Group: Warbler
Size: Up to 11 cm
Call: 'chiff-chaff' song
Summer visitor but winters in western France and around the Mediterranean

The Spotted Flycatcher is another small brown bird with darker upper parts and paler underparts. Look for the dark streaks on its head. Flycatchers are not as secretive as warblers and perch bolt upright. You are most likely to notice one as it flies from its perch to catch a flying insect before quickly returning to perch again. They may build their nest in the ivy on a wall or tree or they may use the old nests of other birds. They lay four or five eggs in a cup of moss and plants, lined with feathers.

Family Group: Flycatcher – Size: Up to 14 cm
Call: Thin, high-pitched 'TSEE'
Also found on the edge of woods – Summer visitor

Robin

You will easily recognize this well-known bird from its orange-red breast and face. Robins in Britain may become quite tame, but birds in other parts of Europe are more secretive. A Robin will defend its territory aggressively, puffing out its red breast as a warning to other Robins to keep away. They feed mainly on insects, and also eat berries and worms. They usually nest in a hollow in a bank or in a hedge, but they have been known to use an old tin can or garden shed. They lay four to six eggs in a deep cup of leaves lined with roots and hair.

Family Group: Thrush
Size: Up to 14 cm
Call: Loud, repeated 'TIC' and song

Willow Warbler

This bird looks just like a Chiffchaff, but some may be much more yellow, especially in the autumn. Willow Warblers have paler legs than Chiffchaffs. In autumn, the Willow Warbler migrates to central and southern Africa for the winter, but in spring and summer it is common all over northern and central Europe. It builds its domed nest of grass and leaves lined with feathers, usually on the ground or almost buried. It lays six or seven eggs.

Family Group: Warbler
Size Up to 11 cm
Call: Song is a series of musical notes trickling down the scale
Summer visitor

Whitethroat

You may see this bird flying from bush to bush while it sings its chattering song. Look for its white throat and reddish brown wings. Females and young have a brown head, but the male has a grey head. Whitethroats build their nests in low brambles and undergrowth. The female lays four to five eggs in the cup of grass.

Family Group: Warbler
Size: Up to 14 cm
Call: Scolding 'CHACK'
Summer visitor

Garden Warbler

The Garden Warbler is similar to the Chiffchaff and the Willow Warbler, but its colour is duller and browner and it scarcely has an eye stripe. Like other warblers, Garden Warblers are hard to spot. They hide in bushes and trees looking for insects. You are most likely to hear them singing a beautiful, tuneful song. The Garden Warbler builds a cup of grasses in low undergrowth to nest in and lays four or five eggs.

Family Group: Warbler
Size: Up to 14 cm
Call: Sharp 'CHECK'
Also found in woods with thick undergrowth
Summer visitor

Pied Wagtail

Their colouring varies considerably, but is always black on the head and shoulders, with white bars on the wings, and a black rump. If you see one that has a grey head or grey shoulders, and a grey rump, it will be a White Wagtail. They mostly eat insects and small seeds. They make their nests of grass and moss lined with hair, in a hole in a bank or ivy-covered wall, where they lay five to six light grey eggs speckled with darker grey.

Family Group: Flycatcher – Size: Up to 18 cm
Call: High-pitched 'CHIZZICK'

Blue Tit

You cannot mistake a Blue Tit with its blue crown and wings, white face and yellow underparts. If you have a bird table, hang a net of seeds from it and you will attract plenty of Blue Tits to feed in your garden. They are very active birds that flit from branch to branch and often hang upside-down to feed. They nest in a hole in a tree or wall, but if you put up a suitable nest-box they may build their nest of moss and grass in it. They lay between six and twelve eggs.

Family Group: Tit
Size: Up to 11.5 cm
Call: 'TSEE-TSEE'

Coal Tit

The Coal Tit is similar to the Great Tit, but smaller and with no yellow on its belly. Look for the buffish white underparts and the white patch on the nape of its neck. It feeds mainly on insects and has a much finer bill than a Great Tit. It uses its bill to probe the needles and cones of conifer trees. Coal Tits sometimes take peanuts from bird tables and hide them. They nest in holes, often in a bank or on the ground and lay seven to eleven eggs in a nest of moss lined with hair.

Family Group: Tit
Size: Up to 11.5 cm
Call: A high-pitched 'P'TWEE-P'TWEE'
Also found in coniferous woods

Wren

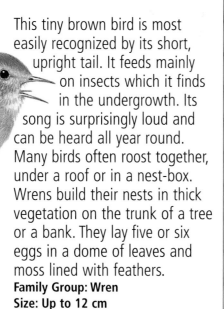

This tiny brown bird is most easily recognized by its short, upright tail. It feeds mainly on insects which it finds in the undergrowth. Its song is surprisingly loud and can be heard all year round. Many birds often roost together, under a roof or in a nest-box. Wrens build their nests in thick vegetation on the trunk of a tree or a bank. They lay five or six eggs in a dome of leaves and moss lined with feathers.

Family Group: Wren
Size: Up to 12 cm
Call: Loud, fast warbling
Also found in woods and hedges

House Sparrow

House Sparrows love to live close to people. You can find them in most towns and cities across the world. Males have a grey crown and black bib. Both males and females have striped brown backs. They eat mainly insects and grain and usually feed on the ground. They like to nest in holes under the roof of a building. They lay three to six eggs in an untidy dome of grass lined with feathers.

Family Group: Sparrow
Size: Up to 14.5 cm
Call: Loud 'CHIRRUP'

Great Tit

Great Tits are larger than Blue Tits. Look for the black head with white cheeks and black stripe through its yellow belly. You are most likely to see Great Tits hunting low down in the trees or on the ground. They use their powerful bills to crush seeds and insects. Like other tits, they nest in holes. They use mainly moss and line it with wool and hair before laying five to eleven eggs.

Family Group: Tit
Size: Up to 14 cm
Call: Song is a loud 'TEACHER-TEACHER'
Also found in woodlands

Dunnock

It is easy to overlook this little brown bird. It is much the same size as a sparrow and has a similar striped brown back, but it has a thin bill and streaky sides. Although it is common in parks and gardens, the Dunnock is a secretive bird. It shuffles along the ground, flicking its tail. It keeps close to hedges or bushes as it looks for insects and small seeds to eat. It builds its nest of twigs, moss and leaves deep inside a bush and lays four or five eggs.

Family Group: Accentor
Size: Up to 14 cm
Call: Loud, high 'TSEEP'
Also found in woods and hedges

Nuthatch

Nuthatches are blue-grey on top and buff underneath. Look for the short tails and the black stripe through their eyes. They feed on insects and nuts, and you are most likely to see them hopping up and down the trunk or branch of a tree. They nest in holes in a tree which they plaster with mud, leaving a hole only big enough for a Nuthatch to squeeze through. Even in a nest-box with the right size of hole, they plaster every crack with mud! They lay five to eight eggs.

Family Group: Nuthatch
Size: Up to 14 cm
Call: Loud 'TUWIT, TUWIT'
Also found in woods

Parks & Gardens

Goldfinch

If this bird is flying you can easily recognize it by the broad yellow band on its black wings. If it is perching, look for its red face as well as the yellow stripe on its wings. Goldfinches are still trapped and sold as caged birds in parts of Europe, but fortunately this is now illegal in Britain. Their favourite food is thistle and teasel seeds. They nest in a thick bush or in the outer twigs of a tree. They lay five or six eggs in a cup of grass and wool.

Family Group: Finch
Size: Up to 12 cm
Call: Twinkling twitter
Also found in open areas with trees

Greenfinch

Greenfinches are less colourful than Goldfinches. Their breasts are brighter green than their backs and wings. Look for the bright yellow patches on their wings and tail. You are most likely to attract them into your garden if you hang some peanuts up for them, although they may drive other birds away from the nut basket. In spring, the males sing as they fly and display their yellow wing patches. Later, their song is more of a wheeze. They nest in shrubs or low trees and lay four to six eggs in a cup of twigs and moss.

Family Group: Finch – Size: Up to 14.5 cm
Call: Musical twitter – Also found in open areas with trees

Hawfinch

The Hawfinch is the biggest finch. It is pinkish brown with black wings. If it is flying, look for the white patches on its wings and at the tip of its short tail. This stocky bird has a big head and huge bill which it uses for cracking open hard seeds like cherry stones. You will be lucky to see this timid bird. In summer, it feeds high up in trees. Even in winter, when it feeds on fallen fruit, it is still difficult to spot. Hawfinches nest in trees and lay three to six eggs in a cup of twigs.

Family Group: Finch – Size: Up to 18 cm
Call: 'TICK', rather like a Robin's
Also found in woods and orchards

Serin

Only male Serins have a yellow head and chest. The females and young are rather drab, but they all have a yellow flash at the base of the tail which you can see as they fly. The Serin has a stout beak and feeds on seeds and insects. It often nests in a coniferous tree and lays three to five eggs in a cup of grass lined with hair.

Family Group: Finch
Size: Up to 11 cm
Call: Fast trill
Not found in Scandinavia; a rare visitor to Britain

Waxwing

This exotic bird is easy to recognize by its pink crest and the red tips on some of its wing feathers. Waxwings breed in the far north of Europe and Asia but move south and west in winter. They may look like Starlings in flight, and often move around in flocks. They nest in small trees and lay four to six eggs in a cup of twigs and moss.
Family Group: Waxwing
Size: Up to 18 cm
Call: Trilling 'shree'
Rare winter visitor to east and north Britain

Chaffinch

The male Chaffinch has a pink breast and blue-grey head. The dull brown female is better camouflaged. When they are flying, look for the white pattern on their black wings. Chaffinches feed mainly on seeds but catch insects in summer. You may see large flocks of them feeding on the ground. They build a nest in a tree or bush and lay four or five eggs in a cup woven of grass and fibres and covered with lichen.
Family Group: Finch – Size: Up to 15 cm
Call: Loud 'PINK'
May also be found wherever there are trees and bushes

Bullfinch

The male Bullfinch is easy to spot with its pinkish red breast. Look for its stout beak and black cap, tail and wings. Bullfinches feed on fruit and seeds, but in spring they turn to buds. They are a pest to fruit-farmers because they spoil the buds on their fruit trees. You will usually see them in pairs although in winter they sometimes form small flocks. They nest in thick bushes and lay four to six eggs in a cup of twigs.

Family Group: Finch
Size: Up to 15 cm
Call: Soft whistled 'DEW'
Also found in woods and hedges

Banquets for Birds

Different birds like to feed in different ways. Some like to feed on the ground, so all you have to do for them is to scatter some food there. Others feed on the seeds of trees and bushes. Birds are most likely to visit your garden if you hang pine cones and other food from your feeder. Here are some ideas for feeding them.

If you live in a flat and do not have a garden, you can make a small feeding point by fixing a strong pole across a window and hanging food from it. There are plenty of birds in even the busiest cities and they will soon get used to you watching them if you keep very still.

Seeds

You can buy wild bird seed from a pet shop, but make sure that it contains grit. Other seeds that birds like include sunflower seeds, millet seeds, and dried sweetcorn kernels.

Don't feed the bird seed sold for caged birds to wild birds because it does not contain the right mixture of seeds.

Coconuts

Ask an adult to help you to drill through one of the eyes of a coconut and drain off the milk. Then ask the adult to saw a section off the other end (about a quarter of its length). Drill another hole through the second eye and thread some wire or plastic string through the holes so that you can hang it up from a branch or the edge of a bird table.

Scraps

Bacon rind, fruit such as apple cores or orange segments, shelled unsalted peanuts, and raisins soaked in water are all good food for birds.

Beware of giving them too many bread or cake crumbs because these fill the birds' stomachs without giving them the energy they need.

Peanut chains

Buy some raw peanuts in their shells. Get some thin wire and string the peanuts on to it by pushing the wire through the middle of the shells. Put about twenty to thirty nuts on each wire and hang them up from a branch or the edge of a bird table.

Alternatively, you can tie the peanuts into a row with a string around their middles. Peanut chains may also attract squirrels.

Pine cone feeders

1 **Collect seven or eight pine cones** (the short, squat sort work best).

2 **Ask an adult to melt 50 grams of lard** in a pan and set it aside to cool.

3 **Stir in 25 grams of natural peanut butter** plus a large tablespoon of plain flour. (The flour is important because it soaks up the grease.)

4 **When the mixture is cool, but still runny**, roll the pine cones in it until all the crannies are filled.

5 **Screw an eye-screw into the stem** of each pine cone, and then use a wire or some string to hang them up from a branch or the edge of a bird table. The pine cones can be refilled when the birds have eaten the mixture.

Suet cake

1 **Melt 50 grams of lard** in a pan. Ask an adult to help.

2 **Stir in 50 grams of wild bird seed**, which you can buy from a pet shop.

3 **Pour the mixture very carefully** into a plastic yogurt or cottage cheese container, large enough to hold it.

4 **Push the end of a piece of string** down through the middle of the container with a skewer. Leave the cake to cool and harden before you remove the container.

5 **Tie the cake to the branch of a tree** or to the edge of a bird table.

Fields, Meadows & Moors

The habitats in this section all have few or no trees. The birds you see here must nest on the ground, either in the open, in long grass, or in gorse or heather. Watch for them feeding on the ground, hopping or walking over the short grass or soil, or in the air, catching insects.

Most birds like to perch on a branch or post to sing, but skylarks and many other birds that live in open spaces sing as they fly. Listen for their songs, then look up to see them high in the sky.

There are lots of different types of open habitats, and you will find different types of birds in each. You will see more birds if there are hedges around the fields and trees nearby. Many birds roost and nest in the trees but feed in the fields.

There are fewer birds on moors and heaths. When you are walking, you may disturb one or two and see them fly up. Look for larger birds overhead or on the horizon. Some birds like the wet, northern moors, and some prefer the dry, sandy heaths in the south. The picture shows nine birds from this book; how many can you recognize?

Curlew, Black Grouse, Hen Harrier, Grey Partridge, Pheasant, Linnet, Red-backed Shrike, Stonechat, Wheatear.

Fields, Meadows & Moors

Short-eared Owl

These owls hunt during the day, so you may see one hovering or gliding low over a field. Notice its long wings and short tail. Look for the black patch at the end of the wing? Short-eared Owls often perch on the ground. Look then for the round yellow face and fierce, yellow eyes. They lay four to eight white eggs in a scrape on the ground. The mother sits on her eggs as soon as they are laid so they hatch out one at a time. Their favourite prey is voles and the number of owlets that survive depends on how many voles there are about.

Family Group: Owl – Size: Up to 38 cm
Call: Hoarse yelp. Song is a hollow 'ʜᴏᴏ-ʜᴏᴏ-ʜᴏᴏ'

Little Owl

This small owl has broad, rounded wings. It hunts mainly at dawn and dusk, but may often be seen in daylight, sitting on a wall or post beside the road with a fierce expression. It feeds mainly on insects, worms and small birds and mammals. It nests in holes in trees or rabbit burrows and lays two to five eggs.

Family Group: Owl
Size: Up to 22 cm
Call: 'ᴋɪᴇᴡ-ᴋɪᴇᴡ', rather like a kitten mewing

Merlin

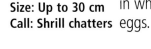

Merlins have streaked reddish underparts. Males are grey above while females are darkish brown. When they are flying, look for their long, pointed wings. Merlins never hover. Instead, they chase and catch small birds, such as Meadow Pipits and Skylarks. These mid-air chases can be long and spectacular. Sometimes Merlins hunt in pairs. They nest on the ground or in a crow's old nest in which they lay three to five eggs.

Family Group: Falcon
Size: Up to 30 cm
Call: Shrill chatters

Barn Owl

These ghost-like owls are sandy-coloured above and white below. They hunt mainly at night, flying over the fields close to the ground on the lookout for rats, mice and shrews. Their numbers are declining, partly due to different ways of farming but also due to poisonous chemicals used on the land. They nest in barns, church towers and holes in trees where they lay four to seven eggs.

Family Group: Owl
Size: Up to 34 cm
Call: Long, eerie screech

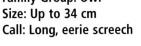

24

Hen Harrier

Male Hen Harriers are silver-grey with white underparts and black wing tips. Females are brown with a barred tail. Look for the white stripe across their rumps. Hen Harriers are becoming more common. You may see one flying close to the ground in a zigzag course across a moorland, hunting for small birds and rodents. They use sticks and grass to build a nest on the ground and lay four to six eggs.

Family Group: Harrier
Size: Up to 50 cm
Call: Usually silent

Black Kite

Black Kites have dark feathers and slightly forked tails. Like other birds of prey, they have sharp talons for catching their prey and hooked beaks for tearing its flesh. They are most common around tree-lined rivers and lakes, but in southern Europe they also scavenge in rubbish dumps and for dead fish along the shore. They make their nest of twigs in trees and lay two or three eggs.

Family Group: Kite
Size: Up to 56 cm – Call: Loud shrill
Summer visitor, but not to Britain and Scandinavia

Red Kite

Red Kites are similar to Black Kites except that their underparts are reddish and their tails are deeply forked. They often glide on their long, bowed wings. At one time, they were common scavengers even in London, but now they are rare. They prey on other birds and small mammals and scavenge dead sheep. They nest in trees and lay two or three eggs.

Family Group: Kite – Size: Up to 70 cm
Call: Mewing notes, first one longer than quickly repeated
Rare in most of Europe

Carrion & Hooded Crows

These large black birds can be seen almost anywhere. Unlike Rooks, you usually see them in ones or twos. Carrion Crows are black all over, but Hooded Crows have grey bodies. You may see birds which are a mixture of the two. Crows eat many foods, like insects, fruit and dead animals. They will also catch small animals and birds and eat eggs. They nest on their own at the top of a tall tree and lay four to six eggs in a cup of twigs.

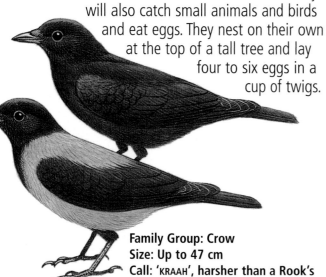

Family Group: Crow
Size: Up to 47 cm
Call: 'KRAAH', harsher than a Rook's

Rook

You will usually see these big black birds in large flocks. You can tell them from Crows by their grey beaks. They probe the ground with their beaks looking for insects, worms and grain. Although farmers consider them a pest, they may actually be helpful by eating insects which are harmful to the crops. They nest together in the treetops in large groups called rookeries. The old nests are easy to see in winter when the trees are bare. Each female lays four to six eggs in a large cup of twigs.

Family Group: Crow – Size: Up to 46 cm – Call: 'CAW'

Magpie

Magpies are easy to recognize from their black and white markings and very long tails. You will usually see them in ones, twos or threes. Watch them as they fly. They give a few fast flaps followed by a short glide. Their domed nests of twigs lined with mud are built in the tops of trees where they lay five to seven eggs.

Family Group: Crow
Size: Up to 46 cm
Call: Cackling chatter 'CACK-CACK-CACK'

Red-backed Shrike

The male Red-backed Shrike has a chestnut back; the female is mainly brown with a speckled breast. It hunts in the same way as the Great Grey Shrike, and has a larder of excess food. It usually builds its nest of small twigs and grass in a thorn bush and lays five or six eggs.

Family Group: Shrike
Size: Up to 17 cm
Call: Sharp, grating 'CHACK' – Rare in Britain: mainly in summer

Great Grey Shrike

You are most likely to see this white and black bird perched on top of a bush or wire. It sits there with only its tail moving, then suddenly swoops down on its prey, a small bird, mammal or insect. It takes its meal back to is perch to eat. Shrikes are also known as 'Butcher Birds' because they store any prey they do not want to eat at once by spiking it on a thorn. Even if you do not see a Great Grey Shrike, you may come across its gruesome larder. It nests in thorny bushes and lays five to seven eggs.

Family Group: Shrike – Size: Up to 24 cm
Call: Harsh 'CHECK' – Rare in Britain: mainly in winter

Jackdaw

Jackdaws often mix with Crows and flocks of Rooks and Starlings, but you can spot a Jackdaw by its black cap and grey nape and cheeks. They feed mainly on insect larvae, but also on young birds, eggs and slugs. They fly with fast wing beats, often acrobatically. They nest in holes in trees, buildings and sometimes in chimney pots. They lay four to six eggs in twigs lined with wool.

Family Group: Crow
Size: Up to 33 cm
Call: Sharp 'chack'

Fields & Moors

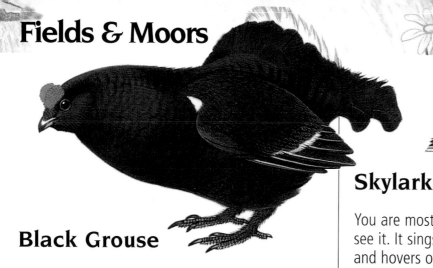

Black Grouse

The best time to see Black Grouse is at dawn by the wooded edge of a moor. Then the males bubble and coo and strut around with their lyre-shaped tails fanned open to show the white feathers underneath. Some have mock battles as the females wait to mate. Black Grouse feed on buds, shoots and berries. When they are flying, look for the male's white wingbars and strangely shaped tail. They nest in a scrape on the ground, which they line with grass, and lay six to eleven eggs.

Family Group: Gamebird – Size: Up to 41 cm
Call: Courting males make bubbling cooing

Willow Grouse

Willow Grouse live on tundra and upland heather moors. They are plump birds with short, rounded wings. If disturbed, they 'explode' from the ground with whirring wings and then glide with wings bowing downwards. They feed on heather shoots and in autumn and winter you may see flocks of them. They nest in shallow scrapes on the ground, which they line with a little grass, and lay five to eight eggs.

Family Group: Gamebird
Size: Up to 40 cm
Call: Harsh
'GO-BACK-
BACK-BACK'

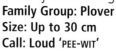

Skylark

You are most likely to hear a Skylark rather than see it. It sings as it rises high in the sky, circles and hovers over its nest. The Skylark's speckled brown feathers make it hard to see against the open ground, but in winter you may see flocks feeding on seeds, worms and insects. Look then for the small crest on top of their heads. The Skylark builds a nest of grass on the ground and lays three to five eggs. In parts of Europe, Skylarks are still shot and eaten as a delicacy.

Family Group: Lark – Size: Up to 18 cm
Call: Loud, clear, warbling song

Lapwing

These birds are easy to recognize when they are standing on the ground feeding on insects, grubs, worms, and snails. Then you can see the tall plumes on their heads. In flight they look black and white. They nest in hollows on the ground and lay four eggs. Like Golden Plovers they will protect their nest by distracting any intruders.

Family Group: Plover
Size: Up to 30 cm
Call: Loud 'PEE-WIT'

Woodlark

Woodlarks are slightly smaller than Skylarks and have white stripes over their eyes which meet at the back of the head. When they fly, look for the black patch on their wings and very short tail. They sing from a perch in a tree or in the air. They feed on seeds and small insects in short grass, and build their nest of grass in a small hollow on the ground often under a bush. They lay three or four eggs.

Family Group: Lark – Size: Up to 15 cm – Call: 'TIT-LOO-EE'

Crested Lark

This lark is easiest to identify by its crest. You may see it on stony or sandy ground as well as in fields, and even on wasteland in towns and on roadsides. It builds its nest of grass on the ground in the shelter of a stone or plant and lays three to five eggs.

Family Group: Lark
Size: Up to 17 cm
Call: Musical 'WHEE-WHEE-OOO'
Not found in Britain and rare in Scandinavia

Golden Plover

Golden Plovers are speckled on top. In summer, they have black underparts, but these become greyish in winter. You will often see them feeding on worms among a flock of Lapwings. They nest in shallow scrapes on open ground and lay four eggs. If the nest is threatened, adults try to lead the intruder away, sometimes by pretending to be injured.

Family Group: Plover
Size: Up to 28 cm
Call: Plaintive 'TOO-EE'
Also found on coast in winter

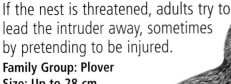

Curlew

You cannot mistake this wader with its long, down-curved bill and long legs. Even if you do not see it, you may hear its distinctive 'curlee' call. Curlews nest on moors, marshes and water meadows. They build their nest in a shallow hollow on the ground often well hidden in heather, and lay four eggs in it. Once breeding is over, many go to the coast and feed on shellfish and lugworms.

Family Group: Curlew
Size: Up to 55 cm
Call: 'CURLEE'
Also found at the coast

Tree Sparrow

Tree Sparrows look much like the familiar House Sparrows, but have a chestnut brown crown and smaller black bib. You may see both in a flock, feeding on grain and insects in a field. The Tree Sparrow's nest is a dome of grass lined with feathers which it builds in holes in trees, walls and farm buildings. It lays four to six eggs.

Family Group: Sparrow
Size: Up to 14 cm
Call: High-pitched 'CHIP-CHIP'

Stonechat

You may see the male Stonechat singing from the top of a bush or on a wire. You can recognize him from his black hood and orange-brown underparts. Look too for the white patch on his neck. Females and young birds are less colourful. Stonechats feed on insects and like to build their nests deep in gorse or heather. The nest is a cup of grass, often with a tunnel to reach it. They lay five to six eggs.

Family Group: Chat
Size: Up to 12.5 cm
Call: Sharp 'TCHACK', like two stones being knocked together

Whinchat

Whinchats are closely related to Stonechats and look very similar, but Whinchats have a white eye stripe and white patches on their tails which only show when they fly. While you may see Stonechats all year round, Whinchats migrate to tropical Africa for the winter. The Whinchat feeds mainly on insects and makes its nest, a cup of grass, by a tussock on the ground. It lays five to seven eggs.

Family Group: Chat
Size: Up to 12.5 cm
Call: 'tic tic'
Summer visitor

Tree Pipit

You will probably hear a Tree Pipit before you see it, and its song is the best way to tell it apart from a Meadow Pipit. Unlike the Meadow Pipit, it prefers ground where there are some trees, and may sing from a perch. Its best song is heard, however, in a song flight like that of the Meadow Pipit. Tree Pipits feed on grasshoppers, beetles and spiders. They hide their nests of grass in a bank or tussock of grass and lay four to six eggs.

Family Group: Pipit
Size: Up to 15 cm
Call: Hoarse 'TEEZ'

Meadow Pipit

Meadow Pipits are the birds you are most likely to see as you walk across moorland in summer. In spring and summer, you can watch their song flight. They rise from the ground with feeble notes which gets faster as they rise and give way to sweeter notes as they fall back to the ground with wings raised and tail spread. They feed on insects and small seeds and hide their nest of grass in a tussock of grass. They lay four to five eggs.

Family Group: Pipit
Size: Up to 14 cm
**Call: Thin 'TSEEP', repeated
two or three times**

Linnet

Linnets are more common than you might think, particularly on farmland, but you will hear them more often than you see them. Look out for the patches of white on the wings and tail as they fly. If you see them perched on wires you should be able to spot the male's red breast and forehead. Linnets feed mainly on seeds of weeds. They often nest together in small colonies, especially in gorse bushes. They lay four to six eggs in a cup of grass and other plants lined with hair and wool.

Family Group: Finch – Size: Up to 13.5 cm
Call: Twittering flight call

Wheatear

Wheatears like to perch on the ground. Look for their white rump and short black tail. In spring, the male has a sandy breast. They feed mainly on insects on the ground. They nest in burrows, stone walls or among stones. They lay five to six eggs in a cup of grass. Wheatears spend the winter in Africa but migrate up to 8,000 km to breed all over Europe and northern Asia.

Family Group: Chat
Size: Up to 15 cm
Call: Hard 'CHACK, CHACK'
Summer visitor

Corn Bunting

It is easy to miss this rather plain bunting when you first start bird-watching, but it is quite common on farmland. Listen out for it in spring and summer singing from its perch on a wire, post or small bush. It has a large head and heavy bill and has no white on its wings or tail. When it flies a short distance, it often leaves its legs trailing down. The Corn Bunting feeds on small seeds and insects. It builds its nest of grass on the ground, often in a cornfield, and lays three to five eggs.

Family Group: Bunting
Size: Up to 18 cm
Call: Song sounds like a bunch of keys being shaken

Ortolan Bunting

Both male and female have yellow necks but only the male has a greenish grey head in spring and summer. They feed on small seeds and insects. They nest on the ground, building a cup of grass lined with hair in which they lay four to six eggs. In the autumn, they migrate to Africa for the winter.

Family Group: Bunting
Size: Up to 16.5 cm
Call: Slow, rich 'TSEE' notes
Summer visitor, rare in Britain

Ring Ouzel

Ring Ouzels look like Blackbirds with a white band across their chests. Females are browner but still have the white crescent. They breed in hilly, moorland country. They feed on insects and berries. They build their nest in heather or in plants overhanging a bank, and lay five to six eggs in a cup of grass.

Family Group: Thrush – Size: Up to 24 cm
Call: Loud 'TCHACK-TCHACK', a clear piping song
Summer visitor

Fieldfare

Fieldfares breed in Scandinavia and central Europe and move south and west in the winter. They have a speckled breast like a thrush, but a chestnut back and grey head and tail. You are most likely to see them in flocks, feeding on insects, worms and berries. In winter, they roost together in thick bushes. They often nest together too. They build their nests of grass and mud in trees and lay four to six eggs.

Family Group: Thrush
Size: Up to 26 cm
Call: Noisy, laughing chuckle 'CHACK-CHACK-CHACK'
Winter visitor to Britain

Redwing

Redwings look rather like dark Song Thrushes (see page 13). Look for the white stripe over the eye and the red on its flanks and under its wings. Listen for its call on autumn nights. Redwings migrate at night as well as during the day. In the morning, you may see them with Blackbirds and Song Thrushes, stripping a hedge of its berries. They breed in Iceland, northern Scotland and Scandinavia. They nest in trees and shrubs and lay five to six eggs.

Family Group: Thrush
Size: Up to 21 cm
Call: Thin, high 'tseep'
Winter visitor
Also found in woodland

Yellowhammer

You are most likely to see Yellowhammers on farmland with thick hedges and trees. Males like to sing their distinctive song from a perch on top of a bush or branch. The female is duller than the male, but still shows some yellow. Look for the chestnut rump and white outer tail feathers as they fly. After nesting, you may see Yellowhammers in flocks with other buntings, finches and sparrows. They feed mainly on seeds but also on insects and fruit. They build their nest, a cup of grass lined with hair, under a bush or in a bank. They lay three to five eggs.

Family Group: Bunting
Size: Up to 16.5 cm
Call: Song 'A-LITTLE-BIT-OF-BREAD-AND-NO-CHEESE'

Corncrake

You may hear the Corncrake's grating call after dark as well as during the day. It sounds like a comb being drawn across a wooden ruler. Corncrakes are very secretive and you will be lucky to catch more than a glimpse of this bird as it skulks in the grass, but look out for its chestnut wings as it flies. It is the only crake you will see in meadows rather than marshes. It feeds on insects and builds its nest of grass in which it lays eight to twelve eggs. In winter, it migrates at night to Africa.

Family Group: Crake
Size: Up to 27 cm
Call: 'CREX CREX'
**Summer visitor,
now very rare**

Fields, Meadows & Moors

Red-legged Partridge

You can recognize a Partridge by its plump body and round head. You can tell the Red-legged Partridge from the Grey by its red legs and its black and white face. They feed on seeds, leaves, roots and young insects. They often gather in flocks and, when alarmed, they run rather than fly away. Their nest is a shallow scrape on the ground lined with plants. Males may build several nests. The female may incubate eight to eleven eggs in one nest but lay another clutch in a second nest for the male to incubate.

Family Group: Gamebird – Size: Up to 34 cm
Call: 'CHUK, CHUKER' – Rare in northern Britain and Ireland

Grey Partridge

To tell a Grey Partridge from a Red-legged, look for its orange-brown face and the dark horseshoe-shaped mark on its belly. They feed on plants on the ground, and can be hard to spot when they are standing still or resting because then they look like large stones. When they are alarmed, they squat down, relying on their camouflage to hide them. Only at the last minute do they fly up into the air. They build their nest on the ground and lay ten to twenty eggs.

Family Group: Gamebird
Size: Up to 30 cm
Call: 'KRRR-ICK', like a swinging rusty gate

Woodpigeon

Woodpigeons are the largest kind of pigeon. They are plump with a smallish head. Look for the white patch on the side of their neck, or, if they are flying, for the white bars across their wings. When they are alarmed, they may crash out of a tree or bush, clapping their wings loudly. They feed on leaves and seeds and in many places are a serious pest to farmers. They build a flimsy nest of twigs in a thick bush or tree and lay three clutches of two eggs. When the birds are young, the parents feed them on a special fluid, called 'pigeon's milk', which is made in the adult's stomach.

Family Group: Dove
Size: Up to 41 cm
Call: Cooing 'oo-ooo-ooo-oo-oo'
Also found in towns

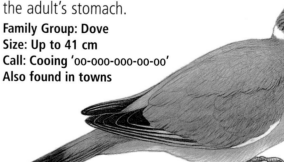

Quail

These small gamebirds are very secretive. Probably the only way you will know they are there is by the male's whistle. They feed on seeds and insects and build their nest on the ground, a shallow hollow lightly lined with grass in which they lay eight to thirteen eggs. In winter, they migrate to Africa, mostly south of the Sahara. Many must die or get shot on the journey, and this may explain why there are fewer of them than there used to be.

Family Group: Gamebird – Size: Up to 18 cm
Call: 'WET-MY-LIPS' – Summer visitor

Stock Dove

It is easy to see that this is a member of the pigeon family. You can tell it is a Stock Dove because it has no white markings. Stock Doves feed on leaves and seeds and you may see flocks of them feeding with Woodpigeons. They build their nests in holes in trees, or in buildings or rabbit burrows. They lay two eggs in their nest which is poorly made with sticks and leaves.

Family Group: Dove
Size: Up to 33 cm
Call: Cooing 'oooo-oo'

Pheasant

You cannot mistake the male Pheasant with his colourful feathers and magnificent long tail. The female has a long tail too, but is less colourful. Pheasants spend most of the day on the ground, looking for grain, seeds, berries, shoots and insects to eat. Notice how they cock their tails when they run. When they fly, they flap their wings violently, then glide. At night, they roost in trees, out of the way of foxes. They make a nest on the ground and line it with plants before laying eight to fifteen eggs in it.

Family Group: Gamebird
Size: Up to 89 cm
Call: 'KAARK-KOK'

Bird Tables

The best place to start bird watching is in your own garden – and the best way to attract birds there is to put out food and water for them. You will have no trouble enticing pigeons, starlings and other common birds to come and feed. In fact, you will probably be surprised by how many different kinds you see. However, you are more likely to get some of the smaller seed-eating birds, such as finches and tits, if you make a bird table.

Simple bird table

1 **Find an old plastic tray** and ask an adult to drill some holes around the edge – one in each corner plus two or three more along each edge will do.
2 **Loop some nylon cord** through the holes at each corner to hang it by. The other holes are to let rainwater drain off.
3 **Hang the bird table from the branch of a tree** as far out of the way of cats and squirrels as you can. Tie the cord firmly.

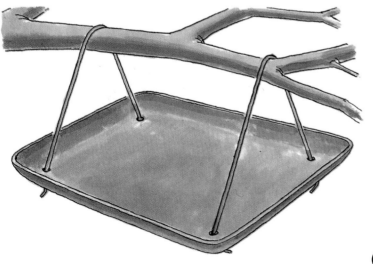

Wooden bird table

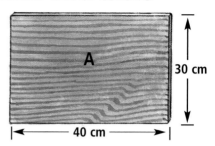

A

30 cm

|← 40 cm →|

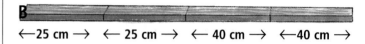

B

←25 cm→   ← 25 cm →   ← 40 cm →   ←40 cm →

You'll need a wooden rectangle about 30 cm x 45 cm (**A**), a strip 130 cm x 2 cm x 2 cm, and a 120 cm post (**C**). If it is to go on a patio, you'll need a wooden plank measuring 280 cm x 6 cm x 2 cm.

1 **Ask an adult to help you saw the strip** into four pieces, two measuring 25 cm long, and two 40 cm long (**B**).
2 **Coat all the pieces with wood preservative** and leave them to dry.

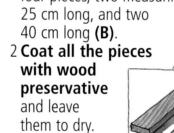

Water

Birds need extra water when the ground is frozen. If it freezes, replace it with fresh water.

At any time of the year, birds will enjoy a bird bath. You can make this quite simply from a dustbin lid, a large potted-plant saucer, or some other wide, shallow basin. If you make sure there is always water in it, the birds will soon know where to come for a drink or a bath.

If you use a dustbin lid, support it with bricks or stones on four sides. Put some small stones in the middle so that the water does not get too deep for small birds.

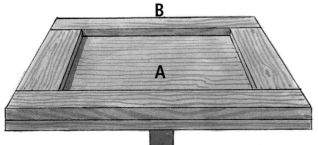

3 **Glue or nail the four strips of wood (B)** on to the rectangle **(A)** as shown. Leave gaps at each corner. These are important because they let rainwater run off and make it easier to clean the tray.

4 **Nail the post (C)** on to the underside of the board in the centre.

5 **For a patio, cut the plank into eight pieces:** four measuring 30 cm long **(D)**, plus four pieces measuring 40 cm **(E)** each.

6 **Nail the four 30 cm strips (D)** to the bottom of the post to make feet. Then nail on the four 40 cm diagonal pieces **(E)** as shown to make the table stand up on its own.

Where to put the table

Before you decide where the table is to go, think about where it will be safest from cats and squirrels. Remember that both are good jumpers. Try to keep it away from shrubs, fences and walls. The second thing to think about is: can you see the bird table from your house? You want to be able to watch the birds without disturbing them.

Looking after your bird table

Once you start putting out food for the birds, make sure you keep doing it. They will expect it! Winter, when the ground is frozen and many of the trees are bare, is when the birds most need extra food. Suggestions for different kinds of food are given on pages 20–21.

Before adding new food, make sure that the tray is clean. If leftover seeds have bird droppings among them, throw the seeds away.

Use warm, soapy water to wash the tray, then rinse and dry it before adding new food.

Mountains

You will have no trouble recognizing a mountain habitat, when you are so high that trees can no longer grow and the ground is covered with scrubby heather or grass and bare rock. You are likely to see more birds on broad, rounded hills where the moorland gives way to cliffs and crags or peat bogs than on sharp, pointed, rocky peaks where there is little cover for birds to nest and not much for them to feed on either.

Look out for birds of prey in the mountains. They feed on smaller birds and small mammals. In the far north, look for mountain birds on low hills and moors too. They are just as cold and bleak as higher mountains further south. The picture shows six birds from this book; how many can you recognize?

Snow Bunting, Dotterel, Golden Eagle, Ring Ouzel, Ptarmigan, Raven.

Water Pipit

You can tell that this speckled brown bird is a pipit from the way it spends much of its time chasing insects on its long legs. It breeds in the mountains in the summer, when it may look quite grey. It builds its grassy nest among waterside rocks and lays four or five eggs. It spends the winter in the lowlands, often by muddy lakes and small streams, but also on the coast.

Family Group: Pipit
Size: Up to 17 cm – Call: 'TSEEP'
Winter visitor to Britain

Snow Bunting

You can identify Snow Buntings from the large amount of white on their heads, underparts and wings. In winter, the male and female have brown backs, but the male has a black back in summer. Snow Buntings never move far from snow and ice. They search through the frozen snow for seeds and insects. Watch them as they feed in flocks. Each bird feeds quickly, runs along the ground, then flies to the front of the flock. They breed in the north of Scotland, Norway, Iceland and Greenland. They nest in the crevice of a rock where they lay four to six eggs in a cup of moss and grass.

Family Group: Bunting
Size: Up to 16.5 cm
Call: Musical 'TEU'
Winter visitor except in the far north
Also on seashores in winter

Ptarmigan

You can tell this is a gamebird by its plump body and small head. In summer, its white wings and underparts show it is a Ptarmigan. In winter, it is all white except for around its eye and the black tail. Ptarmigans feed on leaves, buds and berries of the low plants which grow on high mountain tops. You are most likely to see them near the top of some Scottish ski-lifts. They usually crouch and freeze if alarmed. They nest in a shallow scrape and lay five to eight eggs.

Family Group: Gamebird
Size: Up to 35 cm
Call: Alarm call is a harsh grating sound.

Dotterel

You are most likely to see Dotterels on the tops of the highest mountains, although you may spot them on lower land while they migrate. You cannot mistake the Dotterel's white breast band and chestnut belly. The female has even brighter feathers than the male. They nest on high, exposed ridges. The female lays four eggs which the male usually incubates – he looks after the young when they hatch.

Family Group: Plover
Size: Up to 22 cm
Call: Usually silent
Summer visitor

Mountains

Raven

The Raven is the largest of the crows. Look for the shaggy feathers around its throat. When it is flying, notice how its tail tapers to a point whereas other crows' tails are square. Ravens feed on rabbits, birds and carrion. They have long been associated with death, probably because in the past they hung around battlefields and gallows. They make their nest of twigs in a large tree or on a cliff ledge and lay four to six eggs.

Family Group: Crow – Size: Up to 64 cm
Call: Croaking 'PRRUK, PRRUK'
Also found on sea-cliffs

Golden Eagle

Golden Eagles are much larger and much rarer than Buzzards. If you are lucky, you may see one soaring above a mountain slope, its long wings held in a shallow 'V'. They feed on mammals and birds, especially hares, Ptarmigan and Red Grouse. Like many rare birds, Golden Eagles are protected by law. They build a nest on a cliff or in a large tree and return to it year after year. As they add more twigs each year, the nest can get very large. They lay two eggs which hatch out several days apart, but the older chick usually kills the younger one.

Family Group: Eagle
Size: Up to 80 cm
Call: Usually quiet

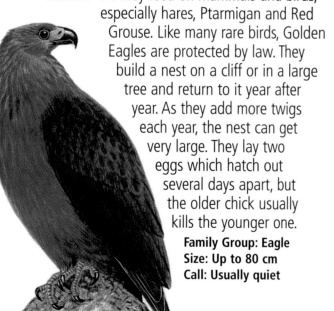

Buzzard

Buzzards are the largest birds of prey that you are likely to see. Watch it soar and hover on broad, rounded wings. Look for its rounded tail and the black patches on its wings. You may also see it perched silently on a fence or a telegraph pole. Look then for its hooked beak. It preys on rabbits and other small mammals and birds, and scavenges dead meat. It builds a nest of twigs in a tree or on a rocky ledge and lays two to four eggs.

Family Group: Buzzards and Hawks
Size: Up to 54 cm
Call: Mewing
Also found on open farmland and coasts

Peregrine

You can tell this bird is a falcon by its long, pointed wings and by the great speed it flies. It is larger than most other falcons and the female is larger than the male. The Peregrine's favourite prey is birds, which it spots from a high perch or when circling in the air. Then it folds back its wings and drops on to the bird at high speed, killing it with its talons. Peregrines do not build a nest, but just lay three to four eggs on the ledge of a cliff.

Family Group: Falcon
Size: 40–46 cm
Call: Chattering 'KEK-KEK-KEK'
Also seen on sea-cliffs

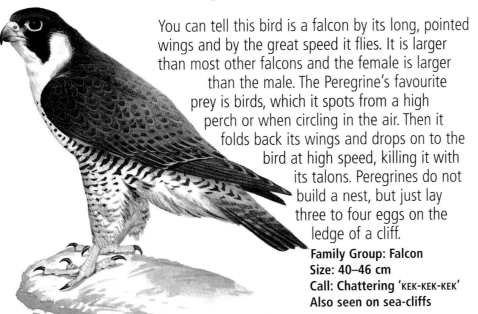

Eagle Owl

This very large owl has large ear-tufts and orange eyes. It lives in forests and wild, mountainous crags and gorges. It hunts mainly at dawn and dusk. It will kill birds as large as Eiders, but it prefers mammals. It will even take foxes and hedgehogs. It nests in small caves or large holes in trees. It lays between two and four eggs.

Family Group: Owl
Size: 65–70 cm
Call: Deep 'OO-HOO'
Never seen in Britain

Chough

You can recognize a Chough (pronounced 'chuff') from other crows by its long, curved red bill. It uses its bill to probe the turf for ants, insect larvae and spiders. The Chough is not as common as other crows, but you may see one flying acrobatically around cliffs or quarries. Its nest is a cup of twigs lined with hair which it builds in a deep rocky crevice or in a small cave. It lays three to five eggs.

Family Group: Crow
Size: Up to 40 cm
Call: Ringing 'CHOW'
Also found on sea-cliffs

Out in the Wild

When you go on a bird-watching expedition, you must dress properly. If it is cold, dress warmly, as you will be spending a lot of time keeping very still. Also, try to wear clothes that do not make a noise as you move. Dress in quiet dull colours that will blend in with the ground and bushes. Dull greens and browns are good. Anything bright will alert the birds. If it has snowed, then of course, white is best.

Take a notebook, pencils, rubber, this book and binoculars with you. You will get the most out of your expedition if you keep a record of what you see. Do your best not to let the birds know you are there. Making a hide for yourself will help.

Making a hide

If you know of a good place to watch birds, but can't get close enough without disturbing them, then why not build a hide for you and a friend?

1 **Find four wooden posts** about 1.5 m long for the uprights, and four strips of wood about 2 m long for the top.

2 **You will also need a piece of canvas** measuring about 5 metres square to cover a hide for two people.

3 **Paint or dye the canvas** with green and brown splotches to camouflage it. Leave a flap for the door and cut out two narrow slits for windows.

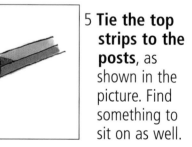

4 **To build the hide**, hammer the upright posts firmly into the ground. Ask an adult to help you with this.

5 **Tie the top strips to the posts**, as shown in the picture. Find something to sit on as well.

6 **Hang the canvas over the top.** Put some large stones around the bottom of the canvas to stop it flapping in the wind.

7 **Leave your hide empty for a day or two** so the birds can get used to it before you use it.

8 **Once you begin using it**, you must always remain very quiet and only talk in whispers. The slightest noise will frighten off any birds around.

Hiding in a car

A car makes a very good hide, too. Be prepared to wait for a little while after the car has stopped for the birds to get used to it. Keep very quiet and still inside. The birds will easily see you through the windows. Roll down the windows a little so that the inside of the glass does not steam up.

Footprints in plaster

In wet weather or after a thaw, look for some clear bird footprints in mud in your garden. You can make a cast of them.

1 **Bend some card into a circle** to make a mould.

2 **Mix up some plaster of Paris** according to the instructions on the box.

3 **Put your mould over the footprint** and pour in the plaster of Paris mixture.

4 **Let the cast harden** before you lift the mould and the plaster.

5 **Wash off the dirt** before you leave the plaster for a few days to set really hard. You can paint or varnish the footprint.

Field sketches

When you see a bird you don't recognize, don't try to look it up in your book. The bird will fly off before you can find it. Instead, make a quick sketch in your notebook with a pencil. You can make a good drawing of the main features by using the simple shapes shown above to draw its outline. Then add the most important details:

- Where are the main patches of colour?
- What shape is its tail?
- Can you see the shape of its beak?

Make a note of what the bird is doing and any other information that will help you to identify it. Now you can look it up in your book.

A field notebook

Use your field sketches as the basis for a field notebook. For each bird you see, write down the date, where you saw it, and what kind of habitat it was in.

If you know the bird already, you can record what it was doing, whether it was alone or in a group and what other birds were nearby.

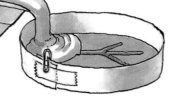

Rivers, Lakes & Marshes

You will always find many kinds of birds near water. The best place to look for them is where the water is still or flows slowly, and where the edges are shallow and muddy and there are plenty of plants. Rivers are not as good as marshes and lakes because the water is often fast-flowing and the banks are steep.

Reservoirs and gravel pits can be exciting places to watch birds too. Both are artificial lakes, but in lowlands, reservoirs may be rich in food and attract many kinds of birds. Marshes are often overgrown with reeds and sedges. Look for rare birds here, such as marsh harriers, bearded tits and bitterns.

Look for waterbirds feeding in different ways. Some feed in open water. Pochards dive deep into the water to find food, but mallards and pintails dabble on, or just below, the surface. Moorhens and herons feed around the edge, while geese and swans graze the grass on the banks.

You will see many waterbirds all year round. In winter, they are joined by swans and geese from the north and in summer by warblers and other birds that have migrated from Africa or the coast. The picture shows twelve birds from this book; how many can you recognize?

Tufted Duck, White-fronted Goose, Marsh Harrier, Heron, Mallard, Moorhen, Pintail, Pochard, Shelduck, Shoveler, Whooper Swan, Reed Warbler.

Rivers, Lakes & Marshes

Kingfisher

Kingfishers like to perch on a branch overhanging a stream or hover just above the water before plunging in to catch a fish. You cannot mistake the bright colours of this little bird. Look for the vivid blue streak on its back and its long bill. You may see it take a fish back to its perch and beat it against the branch before swallowing it head first. They burrow out a tunnel in the bank and lay five to seven eggs in a chamber at the end.

Family Group: Kingfisher – Size: Up to 16 cm
Call: Shrill whistle

Grey Heron

Herons are easy to recognize from their long legs, long neck and dagger-like bill. Notice how they fly with their long necks tucked in. Look for the Grey Heron's grey back and wings and for its wispy, black crest. It often stands, hunched up, on one leg. To feed, it may stand absolutely still in slow water, waiting to stab a passing fish with its sharp bill. Grey Herons also eat small mammals, insects, worms and birds. They build a nest of twigs in a tall tree and lay four to five eggs.

Family Group: Heron
Size: Up to 90 cm
Call: Harsh 'FRAANK'

Marsh Harrier

Reed marshes are the only place you are likely to see this large bird of prey. Look for the broad wings and long tail. Females are brown with creamy heads; males have grey wings and tails and streaked underparts. One male may have more than one mate. Like other harriers, the male sometimes calls a female off the nest. She flies behind and below him to catch the prey which he drops. The prey is usually a water bird or smallish mammal. A Marsh Harrier's nest is a mound of reeds and twigs in which the female lays four to five eggs.

Family Group: Harrier – Size: Up to 52 cm
Call: Usually silent

Coot

Coots are black all over except for their white bills and foreheads. You often see them on the same lakes as Moorhens, but watch how Coots gather on open water and dive below to feed on water plants and insects. If they climb onto land, you will see that the Coot's toes are partly webbed, whereas the Moorhen has long, thin toes. Notice too how Coots fly with their legs trailing down. Coots build a nest of dead waterside plants hidden in reeds and lay six to ten eggs.

Family Group: Rail – Size: Up to 38 cm
Call: Loud, sharp 'KWOK'

Little Grebe

This dumpy little bird is smaller than a Moorhen and is the smallest grebe. Look for its chestnut neck in summer. Like other grebes, you will not often see it flying or walking on land. If it is disturbed, it slips quietly under water perhaps to emerge hidden among water plants. It feeds in shallow water, looking for insects, shellfish and small fish up to two metres below the surface. Its nest is like that of the Great Crested Grebe, but it lays four to six eggs.

Family Group: Grebe – Size: Up to 27 cm
Call: Shrill 'WHINnying' trill

White-tailed Eagle

This large, heavy brown eagle has, as its name tells you, a white tail. It plunges for fish or takes them from the surface of the water. It also hunts seabirds and mammals. It builds its nest of twigs in a large tree or on a cliff. It lays just two eggs.

Family Group: Eagle
Size: Up to 70–90 cm
Call: Loud yelps and yaps
Rare in Britain
Also found on
rocky shores

Moorhen

Wherever there is fresh water, you are likely to see Moorhens. Look for a red and yellow bill and the white line along its flanks. Notice how its head jerks back and forwards as it swims or walks. Moorhens feed on pondweed, berries, snails, insects and small fish. They search the plants that grow around the water for food, and sometimes they come out onto land. They build their nests of plant debris in dense vegetation on the water's edge and lay five to nine eggs.

Family Group: Rail – Size: Up to 35 cm
Call: Throaty 'KIRRICK'

Great Crested Grebe

You will easily recognize this bird in spring and summer from the chestnut frill around its head. It loses the frill in winter, but look for the long, white neck and black crest. Great Crested Grebes dive frequently, often to a depth of four metres below the surface for more than twenty seconds looking for fish. In spring, you can watch them courting. They shake their heads to display their crests. They build a floating heap of plants anchored to other plants as a nest in which they lay three to four eggs. The young are striped white and black.

Family Group: Grebe
Size: Up to 48 cm
Call: Growling
'GORR' but also
barks and moans
Also seen on the sea
in winter

Canada Goose

This is the largest goose and was brought to Europe from North America. Look for the white stripe on its black head and neck. Canada Geese were introduced into large country parks but soon spread. They feed on grass and grain as well as water plants. Their nest is a scrape on the ground which the female lines with her own soft down before laying five to six eggs.

Family Group: Goose
Size: Up to 95 cm
Call: Loud 'A-HONK'

White-fronted Goose

You can tell a White-fronted Goose from a Greylag Goose by its white forehead and the black bars and blotches on its belly. Look too for its orange legs. They feed mainly on grass. White-fronted Geese breed in Russia or Greenland. They nest in a scrape in the ground and lay five to six eggs. Like all geese, they migrate in family groups, so look for some younger geese too. They do not have the white forehead or black bars.

Family Group: Goose
Size: Up to 70 cm
Call: Cackling
Winter visitor
to Britain

Shelduck

These large ducks look a bit like geese. They have glossy green heads and a chestnut band around their breasts. Look for the red knob on the male's bill. When they fly, look for the patch of green on their wings and their black wing tips. Shelducks feed in shallow water, filtering the wet sand or mud for small snails and other shellfish. They usually nest in rabbit burrows in old sand dunes. When the eight to ten eggs have hatched, the parents take the young to feeding areas and leave them in crèches with up to a hundred other young, looked after by only a few adults.

Family Group: Shelduck
Size: Up to 61 cm
Call: Males whistle, females quack
Usually found on sandy or muddy
shores and estuaries

Greylag Goose

This large grey-brown bird has a pale head and heavy, orange bill. Notice too its heavy, pink legs. Like all geese, Greylag Geese often fly in a 'V' formation. They graze on grass and use their large bills to dig up roots. They often nest close together in colonies, each female laying four to six eggs in a scrape on the ground. Domestic geese are all descended from Greylag Geese.

Family Group: Goose – Size: Up to 80 cm
Call: Loud cackling like a farmyard goose

Bewick's Swan

Bewick's Swans are smaller than Mute Swans. Their bills are black and yellow at the base and each one has a pattern of its own. They breed in Arctic Russia, nesting in a mound of plants which they build on the ground. The three to five young mature quickly and are ready to migrate with their parents by the end of the short Arctic summer. Once paired, these swans may stay together for years.

Family Group: Swan
Size: Up to 122 cm
Call: Musical honking
Winter visitor

Whooper Swan

Whooper Swans are as large as Mute Swans; their long yellow bills have black tips too. They breed in Iceland, Scandinavia and northern Russia where they build a mound of plants on the ground and lay five to six eggs. They migrate in flocks and sometimes fly very high.

Family Group: Swan – Size: Up to 152 cm
Call: Loud whooping and trumpeting
Winter visitor

Mute Swan

You cannot mistake a swan with its long, graceful neck and its all-white feathers. To tell one kind of swan from another, you have to look at the bill. A Mute Swan has an orange bill with a black knob at the base. When swans upend, their long necks allow them to reach up to a metre below the water. They feed on water plants and on grass beside the water. If you see swans flying, listen out for the whistling sound their wings make. They build a nest of reeds and other plants on a bank or among reeds. When the five to eight eggs hatch out, the young swans often ride on their parents' backs as they swim. This keeps them warm and safe.

Family Group: Swan
Size: Up to 152 cm
Call: Hisses when threatened

Rivers, Lakes & Marshes

Shoveler

Mallard

Male Shovelers have a green head, and white underparts with chestnut flanks and belly. The females look much like a female Mallard, but look for the patches of green and grey-blue when they open their wings. Notice too their huge, 'shoveler' bills. They sometimes feed together in a circle or line, stirring up the water as they swim to bring more food to the surface. They hide their nest of plants on the ground near water and lay nine to eleven eggs.

Family Group: Duck – Size: Up to 51 cm
Call: Males 'CHOOK-CHOOK', females quack

Pochard

The male Pochard has a chestnut head, black breast and grey back. Females are grey-brown with blotchy cheeks. Look for their short necks and, when they fly, for the pale stripe along their wings. Pochards dive up to three metres deep for their food. They stay under the water for about fifteen seconds, feeding on water plants and small shellfish. They nest on the ground near water or in a reed bed and lay eight to ten eggs in a thick mass of plants.

Family Group: Duck
Size: Up to 46 cm
Call: Occasional growls and wheezes

You may see mallards in any park pond and on almost any stretch of inland water. The male has a green head, a white collar and yellow bill. The female is mottled brown, but both have a purple-blue patch on their wings. They feed by dabbling for food at the surface of the water. They eat seeds, insects and small shellfish. Watch them 'upend' to find food just below the surface. They usually hide their nest on the ground but sometimes build it in a tree. When the nine to thirteen eggs have hatched, the ducklings follow their parents to the water before they are a day old.

Family Group: Duck – Size: Up to 58 cm
Call: 'QUACK' – Also found on sea in winter

Pintail

The Pintail has a longer neck than most ducks which allows it to dabble for food deeper in the water. Look for the male's long, pointed tail. You will see it even when it is flying. Pintails hide their nest on the ground and the female lines it with down before laying seven to nine eggs.

Family Group: Duck – Size: Up to 66 cm
Call: Males whistle, females quack
Winter visitor to Britain

Gadwall

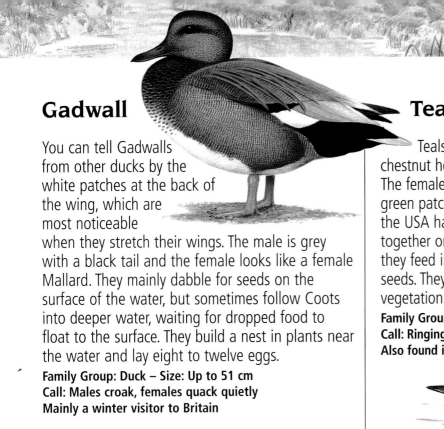

You can tell Gadwalls from other ducks by the white patches at the back of the wing, which are most noticeable when they stretch their wings. The male is grey with a black tail and the female looks like a female Mallard. They mainly dabble for seeds on the surface of the water, but sometimes follow Coots into deeper water, waiting for dropped food to float to the surface. They build a nest in plants near the water and lay eight to twelve eggs.

Family Group: Duck – Size: Up to 51 cm
Call: Males croak, females quack quietly
Mainly a winter visitor to Britain

Tufted Duck

The black and white male has a drooping crest on the back of its head. The female has a smaller crest and is dark brown with pale flanks. Both have a white bar across their wings when they fly. You may see Tufted Ducks chasing midges on the surface of the water, then diving up to seven metres below the surface looking for small shellfish to eat. They build a nest of plants and down, well hidden on the ground, and lay eight to eleven eggs.

Family Group: Duck
Size: Up to 43 cm
Call: Males whistle softly, females growl

Teal

Teals are Europe's smallest ducks. Males have chestnut heads with a green stripe through the eye. The females look like small Mallards – look for the green patches on their wings. Imported birds from the USA have a white line on the breast. They roost together on the water during the day. At night, they feed in shallow water, sifting the wet mud for seeds. They nest on the ground in dense waterside vegetation and lay eight to eleven eggs.

Family Group: Duck – Size: Up to 35 cm
Call: Ringing call (male) and 'QUACK' (female)
Also found in estuaries

Goosander

The male Goosander has a dark green head and black back. Females have a drooping crest and brown head with a white throat. Take a look at their long, thin red bills. They have saw-like edges which help the birds catch and hold onto slippery fish. Goosanders nest in holes in trees or among the rocks. The female lines the hole with down, then lays seven to twelve eggs. The young ducklings often ride on their mother's back.

Family Group: Duck
Size: Up to 62 cm
Call: Usually silent

Dipper

This dumpy little bird likes fast-flowing rivers and streams. Look for its chestnut belly and white bib. Watch it bob on a rock or hunt for insects under the water. It dives or walks along the bottom with its wings spread and looks for food. You can sometimes see the white eyelids winking when the Dipper perches on a rock. It builds a domed nest of moss and leaves, hidden among dense vegetation and lays five or six eggs.

Family Group: Dipper – Size: Up to 18 cm – Call: Loud 'CLINK'

Little Ringed Plover

Look for this bird in gravel pits. Unlike the Ringed Plover, it has a black, white and brown head, but its wings have no white on them. Its long legs are yellow in colour. This Plover feeds mainly on insects. It builds its nest in a shallow scrape on a shingle bank or in a gravel quarry and lays four eggs.

Family Group: Plover – Size: Up to 15 cm – Call: Falling 'PEE-U'
Mainly summer visitor but also found on coasts in winter

Common Sandpiper

Listen for the Common Sandpiper's call and watch it flying low over the water with bowed wings. Look then for the white stripes on its wings. You may also see it bobbing in shallow water as it hunts for insects to snap up with its long bill. In summer, you are most likely to see it near fast-flowing streams and around stony lochs. It builds its nest of plants in a scrape on the ground in which it lays four eggs.

Family Group: Sandpiper – Size: Up to 20 cm
Call: Shrill 'TWEE-WEE-WEE'

Mainly summer visitor but also found on estuaries and coasts in winter

Snipe

Snipe have very long bills which they use to probe deep into the ground in search of worms. Their legs are short for a wader and they have a pale stripe through the crown of their heads. When disturbed, they fly up in a zigzag, calling loudly. In spring, the Snipe flies over its territory making a strange, bleating noise, called 'drumming', with its tail feathers. It nests in wet plates such as rushy fields and upland moors. It lays four eggs in a hollow of plants.

Family Group: Snipe
Size: Up to 27 cm
Call: Harsh 'CREECH'

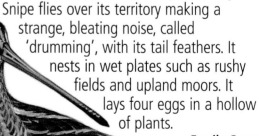

Redshank

Your best chance to see a
Redshank is in the summer
on salt marshes or wet
meadows. Listen for its ringing
call and, if it is flying, look for the broad white band
along its wings. If you can get a close look, notice
its long, orange legs and slender bill. Redshanks
feed in shallow water, searching for insects, shellfish
and worms. They often nest some way from water,
in a shallow hollow lined with grass. When the four
eggs hatch, the young chicks may have a dangerous
journey to get to water.
Family Group: Sandpiper – Size: Up to 28 cm
Call: Loud 'TYU' or 'TEUK' – Also found on coasts

Sand Martin

You will see this brown and white
bird fluttering over rivers, gravel
pits and other stretches of water,
catching flying insects to eat. Its
wings are pointed and its tail is
slightly forked. Look for the band
of brown across its chest. Sand
Martins nest in burrows which
they dig into the side of a bank
and line with feathers. They lay
four or five eggs. In autumn, they
gather to roost in reed beds
before they migrate to Africa for
the winter.
Family Group: Swallows and Martins
Size: Up to 12 cm
Call: Chattering 'CIRRIP'
Summer visitor

Dunlin

You are most likely to see Dunlins on mudflats in
winter. Look for them in groups in winter, standing
with round shoulders, heads down, probing the
mud for worms and shellfish with their long, black
bills. In winter, they have white underparts, but in
spring and summer they have black bellies. In
Britain, they fly to moors to nest in heather or
a grassy tussock where they lay four eggs.
Family Group: Sandpiper
Size: Up to 18 cm
Call: Grating 'ZEE'

Water Rail

Water Rails like wet marshy ground, thick with plants.
You may hear their strange calls, but will find it much
harder to get a good look at them. They skulk among
the reeds looking for insects, small fish, shoots and
roots in the shallow water. They build their nests of
reeds well hidden in the dense vegetation and lay
between six and eleven eggs.

Family Group: Rail
Size: Up to 28 cm
Call: Grunts
and squeals

Bluethroat

This bird is very secretive but you will easily recognize one in summer if you do see it from its bright blue throat and white belly. Young birds and adults in winter do not have the blue patch. Look then for the chestnut patches on the tail. Bluethroats feed on insects and small seeds. They breed mainly in northern and eastern Europe, building a cup of moss and grass on the ground and laying five or six eggs. They migrate to Africa for the winter.

Family Group: Thrush – Size: Up to 14 cm
Call: Sharp 'TAC, TAC' – Rare migrant to Britain

Grey Wagtail

You will usually see the Grey Wagtail along the sides of fast-flowing rivers and streams. Look for its yellow underparts and very long tail. In winter, it may go to slower flowing rivers or even to the coast. Grey Wagtails feed on insects and small water creatures. They build a nest of moss, grass and roots in a hole in the rocks or under a bridge and lay four to six eggs.

Family Group: Wagtail
Size: Up to 18 cm
Call: Sharp 'ZIT'

Yellow Wagtail

You can tell Yellow Wagtails from Grey Wagtails because they are green on top and have shorter tails. You will usually see them in different places. Yellow Wagtails like wet meadows where they feed on insects around the feet of cows and sheep. They are not seen at all in winter. Their nest is a cup of grass built on the ground in which they lay five or six eggs.

Family Group: Wagtail
Size: Up to 17 cm
Call: Loud 'SWEEP'
Summer visitor

Reed Bunting

Reed Buntings look rather like large sparrows. Look for the male's black head and white collar; females are mainly brown. Males and females have broad white sides on their tails. They feed on insects and small seeds. Their nest is a cup of grass and reeds built on or just above the ground. They lay four or five eggs.

Family Group: Bunting
Size: Up to 15 cm
Call: Loud 'TSEU'
Also seen in young conifer plantations and barley fields

Sedge Warbler

The Sedge Warbler has a streaky back and a white stripe over each eye. It likes to nest in the dense waterside vegetation, but you may also see it in drier places, along damp ditches. Sedge Warblers feed on insects and lay five to six eggs in a deep cup of grasses and spiders' webs, built just above the ground. In autumn, they migrate to Africa, making the long journey in a single flight.

Family Group: Warbler – Size: Up to 13 cm
Call: Loud 'CHUCKS' and 'CHURRS' – Summer visitor

Cetti's Warbler

This secretive, dumpy bird is hard to spot. You are most likely to hear it. Its song explodes suddenly and loudly from the bushes around the water's edge. If you see it, look for the pale stripe over its eye. Although Cetti's Warblers feed mainly on insects, they do not migrate in the winter when insects are scarce. One male may pair with several females. They each build a nest of leaves and grass and lay four or five eggs.

Family Group: Warbler – Size: Up to 14 cm
Call: Short 'TIC' or loud 'TSEE'
In England, only in the south and east

Bearded Tit

In spite of its name this bird is not a tit. Listen for it in reed beds where the common reed *Phragmites* grows. You can tell it by its direct, fluttering flight and its long, brown tail. Its favourite food is the seeds of reeds, but it also eats insects, small snails and other seeds. It builds a nest of reeds hidden in dense vegetation and lays five to seven eggs.

Family Group: Parrotbill
Size: Up to 15 cm
Call: Ringing 'PING, PING'
Rare in Britain

Reed Warbler

Warblers tend to be brown on top and paler underneath. Their slim bills are useful for catching insects. Look for the Reed Warbler in thick, wet reed beds. The nest is made from grass and reed flowers and hung from a reed stem. Each female lays between three and five eggs which she incubates as soon as they are laid so that the young do not all hatch out at once. Reed Warblers' nests are often raided by Cuckoos (see page 67) which lay an egg in the nest. When the young Cuckoo hatches, it pushes the other eggs out.

Family Group: Warbler
Size: Up to 12.5 cm
Call: Chacks and churrs
Summer visitor

Long-distance Flyers

You may already be familiar with the comings and goings of robins and blue tits around your home, but look out for different birds in spring and autumn. They may be pausing to rest or feed as they migrate (or move home) from one country to another.

Flying uses a lot of energy, so they need to keep filling up with food. Some species, such as the hawks, swallows and gulls, move in daylight. Most others, including the shorebirds, warblers and orioles, move at night.

Where do they go?

Some birds have quite spectacular journeys. The Arctic Tern travels furthest, from its breeding grounds in the Arctic to spend our northern winter in the Antarctic. In the autumn, the American Golden Plover flies from northern Canada to Argentina. Instead of keeping to the coast, it island-hops across the West Indies. But it rarely stops to rest; it can fly up to 3,200 km without pausing.

Why do birds migrate? Many birds that breed in Britain spend the winters in the warmer south. There they can escape the cold weather. Others may migrate to fresh sources of food, but no one can fully explain the regular movement of some birds in spring and autumn.

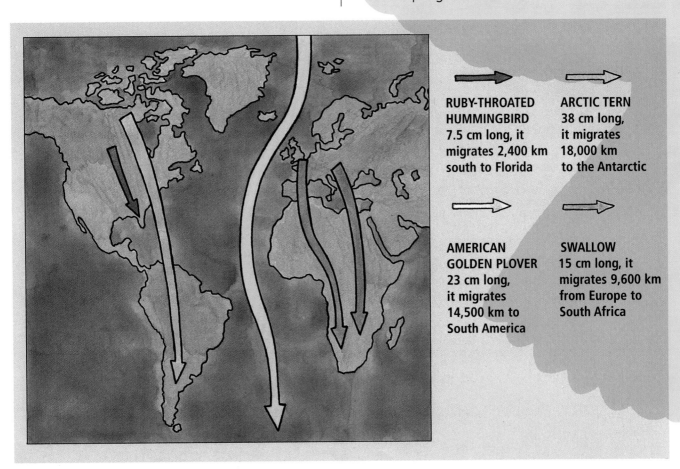

RUBY-THROATED HUMMINGBIRD
7.5 cm long, it migrates 2,400 km south to Florida

ARCTIC TERN
38 cm long, it migrates 18,000 km to the Antarctic

AMERICAN GOLDEN PLOVER
23 cm long, it migrates 14,500 km to South America

SWALLOW
15 cm long, it migrates 9,600 km from Europe to South Africa

Finding their way

How birds migrate is even more mysterious, but they probably use the sun or the light of the stars to find their way. Many birds migrate up the coast. This is safer than flying across oceans and probably helps them to stay on course. But on foggy nights they may become confused by the long flashes of lighthouses and fly straight towards them. To stop birds flying into them, some light houses have changed to using short flashes only.

Bird warning

Migrating birds that are just passing through can be confused by large windows. They may try to fly through them and stun themselves. You can help by hanging a warning in your window. A hawk shape works well because most birds keep well away from hawks.

1 **Trace the hawk shape** on this page on to a piece of thin paper with a pencil.
2 **Glue it on to a large piece of thin card** – an old cereal packet will do. Carefully cut around the edges with scissors.
3 **Colour the hawk shape black** using a crayon or paint. The blacker you can make it, the better.
4 **Attach about 60 cm of string** to the head of the hawk with sticky tape and use a drawing pin to attach it to the top of your window frame.
5 **If you can attach it to the outside of your window** it will move about in the wind and look more realistic. But first cover it in plastic to protect it from the rain. If you use black plastic, it will save you colouring in the shape.
6 **You can also hang glittering or tinkling objects** in a problem window. Tape long streamers of tin foil to the top of the frame or hang up some wind chimes.
7 **Or you could attach some light, see-through material** over the glass to reduce the reflections. This need only be up during the danger periods in the spring and autumn.

Woodlands

Trees provide plenty of places for birds to roost and nest and plenty of food for them to eat. Woods ring with the calls and songs of birds, but the birds themselves are often hard to see. They are well hidden among the leaves.

Most birds live at the edges of woods or clearings, rather than deep inside the dark forest. Woods with broad-leaved, deciduous trees have more birds than conifer woods. Old, natural conifer woods will have more birds than commercial plantations. However, there are some birds that thrive in conifer woods, especially those with clearings. Look for goldcrests and crossbills here.

The best woods for birds are those with many kinds of trees, bushes and other plants. Some birds, such as nightingales and song thrushes, like the thick undergrowth or search for food among the rotting leaves on the ground. Others prefer to feed and nest in upturned tree roots or fallen branches. Woodpeckers and treecreepers hunt on the trunks and bigger branches of the trees themselves, but birds such as golden orioles and redpolls keep to the treetops and are hard to spot.

Spring and summer are the best times to see woodland birds, but you have to be very patient. Sit quietly on the edge of a wood or a clearing and wait for the birds to show themselves. Try to get to know their songs and calls. Remember that you will see many garden birds in woodlands. The picture shows eleven birds from this book: how many can you recognize?

Cuckoo, Pied Flycatcher, Goldcrest, Jay, Nightingale, Golden Oriole, Siskin, Sparrowhawk (female), Crested Tit, Treecreeper, Great Spotted Woodpecker.

Woodlands

Sparrowhawk

The Sparrowhawk has broad wings, a long tail and barred underparts, the female's underparts being much paler. It preys on flocks of small birds along hedges or at the edge of a wood. It often uses the cover of trees and bushes to get close to them before making a sudden dash after the slowest one. It gives chase, beating its short wings very fast, until it catches the small bird in a large, yellow foot and carries it away to pluck it and eat it. Sparrowhawks build nests of twigs in trees and lay three to five eggs.

Family Group:
Hawk
Size: Up to 30 cm
Call: Loud
'KEK-KEK-KEK'

Honey Buzzard

The Honey Buzzard has longer wings and a shorter tail than the much smaller Sparrowhawk. Look for the dark bands on its tail. You are most likely to see it in clearings and at the edge of forests. This bird gets its name because it feeds by digging out wasps' and bees' nests, but it actually eats grubs rather than honey. Honey Buzzards also eat frogs, small birds and mammals. They make a nest of twigs in a tree and lay two eggs.

Family Group: Honey Buzzard
Size: Up to 55 cm
Call: Usually quiet
Summer visitor but rare in Britain

Goshawk

Goshawks are larger than Sparrowhawks, but look similar in the air. They are rare in Britain and were once extinct in the wild, but a few have escaped from falconers and you may see them in some large woods. They prey on Woodpigeons, Crows and small mammals. They may watch from a perch then give chase, flying fast and low to catch their prey. They build their nest of twigs in a tree and lay three or four eggs.

Family Group: Hawk
Size: Up to 50 cm
Call: 'KEK-KEK-KEK', louder and harsher than a Sparrowhawk's

Tawny Owl

Tawny Owls hunt at night. They watch from a perch then drop down onto a mouse, small bird, frog or even a worm. During the day, they roost in holes or in trees. You may see one being mobbed by a flock of small birds, trying to warn others of its presence. The Tawny Owl is dark brown above and below and has a large round face with black eyes. Like other owls, both eyes point forwards. They nest in a tree hole in which they lay two or three eggs.

Family Group: Owl
Size: Up to 38 cm
Call: 'KE-WICK'; song is the well-known 'HOOO-OOO-OO-OOOO'
Also heard in parks and towns

Long-eared Owl

The two tufts of feathers on the Long-eared Owl's head are not ears. They are always held flat when flying but are raised when the owl is nervous. This owl is not as stout as a Tawny Owl and its eyes are orange. It hunts at night and is hard to see. Long-eared Owls prey on small mammals, birds and insects. You may hear them in conifer plantations where twelve or more owls may roost together in winter. They usually take over the old nest of a crow or other bird and lay three to five eggs.

Family Group: Owl
Size: Up to 36 cm
Call: Soft, moaning 'oo-oo-oo'

Nightjar

Family Group: Nightjar
Size: Up to 27 cm
Call: 'CHUCK', song a loud 'CHURRING' usually made after dark
Summer visitor

You are more likely to hear this speckled bird than to see it. It can sing for a long time on summer evenings. Listen too for its 'CHUCK' as it flies. Nightjars feed on moths and other insects, caught in mid air at night. Look for their long wings and long tail as they twist and turn in the air. During the day, they perch on the ground or along the branch of a tree, but their grey and brown feathers camouflage them. They lay two eggs on the ground without building a nest. In winter, they migrate to Africa.

Woodlands

Capercaillie

Capercaillies are the largest European gamebirds. The male is dark grey and the smaller female is striped brown. In spite of their size, they are hard to spot in the pine forests and conifer plantations where they live. These secretive birds feed on shoots and buds of conifer trees and on berries. For a few weeks in spring, males gather in the early morning to sing and fight. They display to the many females who come to watch. Females build a nest on the ground, lined with plants, in which they lay seven to eleven eggs.

Family Group: Gamebird – Size: Up to 86 cm
Call: Various noises including pops,
drums rolls, brays and cackles
Rare in Britain: only found in the north

Woodcock

This bird looks similar to Snipe and other waders of marshy land, but it is larger and plumper. Woodcocks have long bills with which they probe the ground for worms. They have short legs and their mottled feathers camouflage them against the trees and undergrowth. The best time to see Woodcocks is at dusk in early summer. Look for them flying low over the woods and calling 'TSIWIK'. They are trying to attract a female. They build a nest in a shallow hollow on the ground and line it with dead leaves before laying four eggs.

Family Group: Wader – Size: Up to 34 cm
Call: Sharp 'TSIWIK' and deep croak

Turtle Dove

It is easy to recognize this bird as a pigeon although it is more slender than most. Look for the mottled reddish brown patches on its wings. Listen too for its soothing, purring song in thick hedges and near the edge of woods. Turtle Doves feed on leaves and seeds and build a flimsy nest of twigs in a bush or hedge. They lay two clutches of two eggs before migrating in autumn to West Africa.

Family Group: Dove
Size: Up to 27 cm
Call: Loud, musical purring
Summer visitor

Black Woodpecker

This is the largest woodpecker in Europe. Look for its black feathers and the male's red crown. The female has just a small red patch on the back of her head. You are most likely to come across them in conifer woods. They feed on insects in the trees and drill a nest hole in which they lay four to six eggs.

Family Group: Woodpecker
Size: Up to 45 cm
Call: Loud whistles and yelps, ringing 'KREE-KREE-KREE'
Never seen in Britain

Lesser Spotted Woodpecker

This small woodpecker is no larger than a House Sparrow. Only the male has a red crown. Its main food is insects which have bored into wood. It catches them with its long tongue. Lesser Spotted Woodpeckers drum like the Great Spotted Woodpecker, but their drumming is higher pitched. They drill out a nest hole in old wood, often on the underside of a branch and lay four to six eggs.

Family Group: Woodpecker
Size: Up to 15 cm
Call: Shrill 'KEE-KEE-KEE'
Also found in large gardens

Great Spotted Woodpecker

Unlike Green Woodpeckers (see page 10), you will hardly ever see Great Spotted Woodpeckers on the ground. You can tell the Great Spotted Woodpecker by the large patches of white on the shoulders and the red under the tail. Look for these features if you see it hopping up a tree. Notice its long, strong bill and the way it holds its tail stiffly against the bark for extra support as it moves. It feeds on insects, nuts, seeds and berries. In spring, you will hear the male drumming loudly. It is not drilling its nest hole, but asserting its territory. Male and females chip out a nest hole for the four to seven eggs.

Family Group: Woodpecker
Size: Up to 23 cm
Call: Sharp 'CHICK' or 'KECK'
Also found in parks and gardens

Woodlands

Redstart

Redstarts get their name from their red tails which they often flick and quiver. Males also have reddish underparts. Females have no black and are buff underneath. Redstarts feed mainly on insects. Males often catch theirs in the air, but females prefer to feed on the ground. They build their nest of moss and grass in a hole in a tree or wall and lay five to seven eggs.

Family Group: Thrush
Size: Up to 14 cm
Call: 'hveet'; song is warbling
Summer visitor
(See also Black Redstart, page 12)

Golden Oriole

Although the male is vivid yellow, these birds are so secretive you will be lucky to catch more than a glimpse of them among the treetops. The females are greenish and may be confused with Green Woodpeckers but they do not have a bounding flight. Golden Orioles feed on insects and in autumn on fruit. Their nest is a cup of woven grass and bark, slung between two twigs at the very end of a branch. They lay three or four eggs. In autumn, they migrate to central and southern Africa.

Family Group: Oriole – Size: Up to 24 cm
Call: Song is a flute-like 'WEELA-WEEOO'
Summer visitor but scarce in Britain

Crossbill

Look for these birds in conifer forests, especially those with plenty of spruce trees. The male is red with brown wings and tail. The female is olive green. They feed on the seeds inside cones. They grip the cone with their feet, and then use their strange, crossed bills to prise out the seeds. They nest in a small cup of twigs lined with grass and hair which they build at the top of a tree. They lay three or four eggs.

Family Group: Finch
Size: Up to 16.5 cm
Call: Loud 'CHIP, CHIP, CHIP'

Treecreeper

This small bird is brown on top and white underneath. Watch it as it feeds. It starts at the bottom of the trunk and climbs up and around it until it reaches the thinner branches. Then it flies to the bottom of another tree to start again. Notice its long downward-curving bill which it uses to probe the bark for insects. It builds its nest of twigs and moss behind a split in the bark and lays five or six eggs.

Family Group: Treecreeper
Size: Up to 12.5 cm
Call: High-pitched 'TSEE'

Mistle Thrush

You can recognize this bird as a thrush from its speckled breast. It is larger than a Song Thrush and the whole of its underwing is white. Mistle Thrushes feed on insects, worms and berries. In autumn, they fly around in noisy flocks looking for bushes or trees with berries. When a storm is looming, most birds stop singing and take cover, but Mistle Thrushes keep on singing loudly, which is why country people used to call them 'Stormcocks'. They build their nest of grass or moss in the fork of a tree and lay three to five eggs.

Family Group: Thrush
Size: Up to 27 cm
Call: Chattering rattle, its song is rather like a Blackbird's
Also found in parks

Nightingale

You may find it hard to spot this reddish brown, secretive bird, but, if it is around, you can hear its beautiful song at any time of the day or night. Listen just before dawn or after dusk when other birds are quiet. Nightingales spend most of their time in thick bushes or on the ground hunting for worms, spiders and insects. They build a nest of leaves hidden in thick undergrowth on or near the ground and lay four to six eggs. They migrate to central Africa for the winter.

Family Group: Thrush
Size: Up to 16 cm
Call: Loud, rich song with many rapid phrases
Summer visitor

Wryneck

This small brown bird is called Wryneck because of the way it twists and turns its head. If you get a close look at it, notice the arrow-shaped mark on its back. It feeds on ants and other insects. It nests in a hole in a tree or in a nest-box and lays seven to ten eggs.

Family Group: Woodpecker
Size: Up to 16 cm
Call: Repeated 'KEEU'
Summer visitor, rare in Britain

Woodlands

Wood Warbler

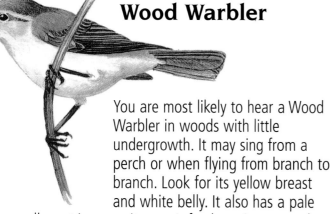

You are most likely to hear a Wood Warbler in woods with little undergrowth. It may sing from a perch or when flying from branch to branch. Look for its yellow breast and white belly. It also has a pale yellow stripe over its eye. It feeds on insects and builds its nest on the ground, a dome of grass and leaves, in which it lays five to seven eggs. It migrates to Africa for the winter.

Family Group: Warbler – Size: Up to 12.5 cm
Call: Either 'PIP-PIP-PIP' getting faster and faster,
or repeated 'PEE-OU' – Summer visitor

Firecrest

Firecrests look much like brighter Goldcrests except that they have a white stripe over each eye. They too like old conifer forests. They feed on insects and, like Goldcrests, build their nests of moss and spiders' webs at the tip of a branch. They lay seven to nine eggs.

Family Group: Warbler
Size: Up to 9 cm
Call: 'ZIT, ZIT'; song similar to Goldcrest
but much simpler 'ZI-ZI-ZI-ZEEE'
Scarce in Britain

Pied Flycatcher

Male birds are black and white in spring and easy to spot, but in autumn they look more like the brown and white females. These small birds feed on flying insects. They nest in a hole in a tree or in a nest-box. They line it with leaves and lay five to eight eggs.

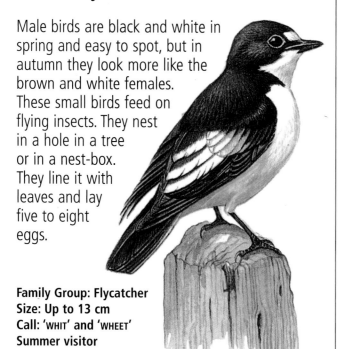

Family Group: Flycatcher
Size: Up to 13 cm
Call: 'WHIT' and 'WHEET'
Summer visitor

Goldcrest

The Goldcrest is quite common in conifer woods, but is difficult to spot. Sit quietly and listen for its song, then try to see it. It is a tiny, dumpy bird with a yellow and black or orange and black crown. It feeds on insects and often hovers or hangs upside-down to pick them from under the needles. It makes its nest of moss woven together with spiders' webs at the tip of a branch. It lays seven or eight eggs.

Family Group: Warbler
Size: Up to 9 cm
Call: High 'see'; song is
'TIDDLE-DE-EE, TIDDLE-DE-EE,
TIDDLE-DE-EE'

Lesser Whitethroat

It is easy to miss this bird, with its white throat and dark cheeks. Lesser Whitethroats are secretive birds which hunt for insects in thick bushes or hedges, especially in hawthorn. They build a nest of twigs and grass low down in a bush and lay four to six eggs. Listen out for the adults' calls as the fledglings leave the nest.

Family Group: Warbler – Size: Up to 13.5 cm
Call: Sharp 'tac', song is a rattle – Summer visitor

Blackcap

You are most likely to hear this small bird in woods with thick bramble bushes or other undergrowth. Look for the male's black cap and the female's brown one. They feed on insects and berries. In winter, they usually migrate to southern Europe and North Africa, but you may see a few of them feeding from bird tables. Their nest is a cup of plant stems which they hide in nettles or brambles and in which they lay four or five eggs.

Family Group: Warbler
Size: Up to 14 cm
Call: Sharp 'CHACK', song is a rich, clear warble
Mainly summer visitor

Cuckoo

Family Group: Cuckoo
Size: Up to 33 cm
Call: 'CUCK-OO'
Summer visitor

Listen for the Cuckoo's well known call in spring, on moorlands and in reed beds as well as in woodlands. It looks rather like a hawk, with its long tail, grey back and striped underparts, but look for its pointed wings and small head. Cuckoos feed mainly on hairy caterpillars and other insects. After mating, the female looks for the nest of a small bird, such as a Dunnock, Reed Warbler, Wren or Meadow Pipit, and lays an egg in it. She then carries away one of the other eggs. The young Cuckoo usually hatches first and quickly pushes out all the other eggs so that its small foster parents feed only it. The female Cuckoo lays up to twenty-five eggs, putting each in a different nest. In autumn, Cuckoos migrate to central or southern Africa.

Woodlands

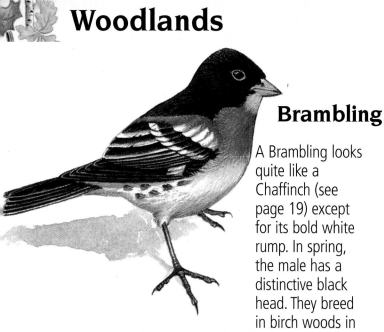

Brambling

A Brambling looks quite like a Chaffinch (see page 19) except for its bold white rump. In spring, the male has a distinctive black head. They breed in birch woods in northern Europe. They feed on insects and build a nest of grass, lichen and strips of bark in a tree. They lay five to seven eggs. In winter, they prefer to live in beech woods where their favourite food is beech mast (beech nuts).

Family Group: Finch – Size: Up to 14.5 cm
Call: Harsh 'TSWARK' – Winter visitor to Britain

Siskin

This greenish yellow bird is streaked with black and has yellow on its wings and tail. The male has a black cap and chin. Look for it in summer in woods with plenty of conifers and birch trees. In winter, you are more likely to see it along with Redpolls in alders growing beside rivers. Siskins feed on seeds, often hanging onto the thinnest twigs to reach their food. They will also feed on peanuts hung from a bird table. Their nest is a small cup of moss and twigs which they build high in a conifer and in which they lay four or five eggs.

Family Group: Finch
Size: Up to 12 cm
Call: Clear 'TSUU'

Redpoll

You may see this small, streaked bird feeding on small seeds at the tops of birch or alder trees. Look for its red forehead and black chin. It seems to bounce as it flies from tree to tree. Look for the two buff bars on its wings when it settles. Its nest is a tiny cup of plant debris covered with lichen. It builds it in a small tree and lays four to six eggs.

Family Group: Finch – Size: Up to 13.5 cm
Call: 'ZZZ-CHI-CHI-CHI' while flying

Nutcracker

This brown bird is spotted with white and has a patch of white under its tail. It lives in conifer forests in high mountains where it feeds on conifer seeds and hazelnuts. It builds a large, untidy nest of moss and twigs in a tree and lays three or four eggs. In winter, it may move lower down the mountains into broad-leaved woods.

Family Group: Crow
Size: Up to 32 cm
Call: Harsh cries
Very rare visitor to Britain

Crested Tit

This bird is easy to recognize in the old pine forests where it lives, by its speckled black and white crest. Look too for the black 'C' on its face. Crested Tits feed on insects and seeds. The female digs out a nest hole in the rotten stump of a tree but she will also use a nest-box. The nest is made of moss lined with hair in which she lays five to eight eggs.

Family Group: Tit
Size: Up to 11.5 cm
Call: Quiet 'SI-SI-SI'
and soft 'CHURR'
In Britain, found only
in Scottish Highlands

Long-tailed Tit

Look for this tit where you hear its calls. You will easily recognize it by its tiny, round body and long tail. When they are not breeding, Long-tailed Tits move around in flocks with other birds such as Goldcrests, Blue Tits, Treecreepers and Chaffinches. Together they search the woods and hedges for small insects to eat. Long-tailed Tits build a large, domed nest of moss, spiders' webs and lichen, lined with up to 2,000 feathers. They lay between eight and twelve eggs. Other Long-tailed Tits will help to feed the chicks when they hatch.

Family Group: Tit – Size: Up to 14 cm
Call: 'TSEE-TSEE', also 'TSRRP' when in a flock

Marsh Tit

In spite of its name the Marsh Tit is seldom seen in marshes. It actually prefers even drier broad-leafed woods than Willow Tits do. Marsh Tits are often seen with Willow Tits and it is hard to tell them apart. Both have black caps, brown backs and buff underparts. They feed on insects and small seeds. Marsh Tits keep the same mate until one dies. It is then quickly replaced. They nest in holes in trees using moss lined with hair or fur. They lay six to eight eggs.

Family Group: Tit
Size: Up to 11.5 cm
Call: Loud 'pitchou' and
scolding 'CHICKA DEE-DEE-DEE'
Sometimes found in gardens

Willow Tit

The best way to tell a Willow Tit from a Marsh Tit is by its call. If you can get a close look at it, you may notice that its throat is more untidy than a Marsh Tit's. They feed on insects and seeds, and they often prefer damp woods at breeding time. Each year, the female digs out her own nest hole in rotten wood and makes a nest of wood chips and plant fibres. She lays six to nine eggs.

Family Group: Tit
Size: Up to 11.5 cm
Call: Wheezy
'EEZ-EEZ' or
harsh 'CHAY'

Helping Birds in Danger

The best way to help endangered species is to join a wildlife group that is working to save them. As well as donations they need as many people as possible to become aware of the problems. You can help by explaining the problems to other people.

Get involved

Find out whether there is a local group involved in wildlife conservation. If you join them, you can help with fund-raising and other activities.

1 **Listen out for particular issues.** Is there a local area of land important to wildlife which is being threatened by building work? As towns grow, woods may be cut down and marshes drained to make more land available for building on.
2 **You can write** to your local MP and to your local government councillor asking him or her to help your cause and [on] conservation generally.
3 **Visit as many bird sanctuaries as possible.** You can not only enjoy seeing the birds, but you will also see what is being done to help them.

First aid

If you find a bird that has been stunned or hurt by flying into a window, take it indoors and place it in a medium-sized box with a lid. Don't handle it any more than you have to. After a few hours' rest, it will probably have recovered enough for you to let it go. For more serious injuries, call your local vet for advice.

If you find a chick helpless on the ground, but alive, what should you do?

1 **Don't touch it** until you have watched and listened to check whether the parents are nearby, looking after the chick from a distance.
2 **When you are sure they are not, then make a nest for the bird** in a small box with shredded kitchen towels or tissues. Keep it very quiet. Then call the local wildlife society or RSPB officer (see page 78) to ask what to do.

Rescuing an oiled bird

A particular danger for sea birds is oil, either spilt by accident or emptied by tankers into the sea. Once a bird's feathers are covered in oil, it cannot swim or fly, so it cannot catch food and will soon starve to death. Even a small amount of oil can do a lot of harm. If the bird tries to clean itself by preening, it may swallow enough oil to kill it.

If you find a live bird covered in oil, do not try to clean it yourself. Contact a local bird group or vet who will know how to deal with it.

Keeping track

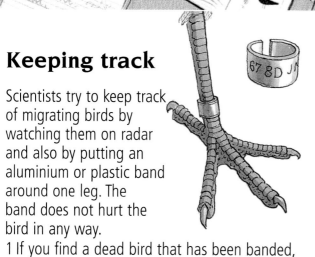

Scientists try to keep track of migrating birds by watching them on radar and also by putting an aluminium or plastic band around one leg. The band does not hurt the bird in any way.

1 If you find a dead bird that has been banded, **take the band off its leg**.
2 **Post the band** to the address given on it.
3 **Enclose a note** about when, where and how you found the dead bird.

A bird-friendly garden

You can make your own small bird sanctuary in your garden with an adult's help.

1 **Ask if you can plant trees and shrubs** that birds particularly like. Elder, dogwood, hawthorn, cotoneaster and holly are good ones to begin with. Any tree or shrub with fruit or berries will soon bring birds into your garden.
2 **Ask if you can have a special corner** where you can let weeds grow. Rye grass, plantain and even ragweed all have seeds that birds like to eat.
3 **Marigolds will attract birds** if their flower heads are left to go to seed in autumn.
4 **Watch the birds carefully.** Which plants do they visit most? Which ones do they ignore? You will know which ones to keep next year!
5 **If you plant thick climbing plants**, such as honeysuckle and ivy, you may find birds nesting in them too.

Seashores

There are many kinds of coastline, from rocky cliffs and sandy or shingle beaches to muddy estuaries – each attracts different kinds of birds.

When you think of seabirds, you probably think of gulls. Herring gulls nest on rocky cliffs and are impossible to miss as they wheel noisily overhead. But rocks and cliffs provide nesting sites for other birds like guillemots, cormorants and kittiwakes. Out to sea, there may be ducks, grebes and shags, but they can be hard to spot among the waves. Watch for gannets and terns diving for fish.

Look for gulls, terns and plovers on sandy and shingle beaches. In winter, wading birds such as turnstones come to feed along the shoreline. Saltmarshes, brackish lagoons and estuaries will attract many more birds than an exposed beach. In winter, you will see waders, geese and ducks there. The picture shows eight birds from this book; how many can you recognize?

Fulmar, Guillemot, Great Black-backed Gull, Herring Gull, Kittiwake, Oystercatcher, Shag, Common Tern, Dunlin.

Bar-tailed Godwit

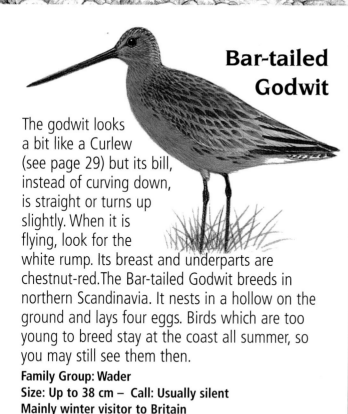

The godwit looks a bit like a Curlew (see page 29) but its bill, instead of curving down, is straight or turns up slightly. When it is flying, look for the white rump. Its breast and underparts are chestnut-red. The Bar-tailed Godwit breeds in northern Scandinavia. It nests in a hollow on the ground and lays four eggs. Birds which are too young to breed stay at the coast all summer, so you may still see them then.

Family Group: Wader
Size: Up to 38 cm – Call: Usually silent
Mainly winter visitor to Britain

Oystercatcher

It is easy to spot this black and white bird with its long orange bill and pink legs. In spite of its name, the Oystercatcher does not eat oysters! It uses its strong bill either to stab or to prise open the shells of mussels, cockles and limpets. Its nest is usually a shallow scrape which it scratches in the sand or shingle. It lays two to four eggs. Sometimes it comes inland to breed, in gravel workings or reservoirs. Then it feeds on worms.

Family Group: Oystercatcher
Size: Up to 43 cm
Call: Loud 'CHIP-CHIP'
May also be found on fields inland

Turnstone

This stocky bird is dark on top and light below. In summer, its back is chestnut red and its head is white. You can clearly see its black and white markings when it flies. Turnstones feed on creatures which live under stones. Watch them use their short, stout bills to probe under the stones or even turn them over, as their name implies. They breed in northern Europe and Greenland where they lay four eggs in a shallow hollow on open ground.

Family Group: Wader
Size: Up to 23 cm
Call: Twittering 'KITITITIT'
Mainly winter visitor to Britain

Ringed Plover

This brown and white bird has black on its face and a broad, black collar. Look too for its orange legs and bill and for the white stripes on its wings when it flies. Watch for it feeding. It may patter the wet mud with its feet, mimicking the sound of rain on the ground to bring worms up to the surface. It may dart forward to seize a worm or mollusc it has seen. Its nest is a shallow scrape in the shingle in which it lays four eggs.

Family Group: Plover
Size: Up to 19 cm
Call: 'TOO-LEE'
Sometimes nests inland

Seashores

Puffin

It is easy to recognize a Puffin in summer from its colourful, triangular bill. In winter, it sheds the outer plates, leaving a smaller, black bill. Puffins dive underwater for fish and can hold up to ten in their bill at once. Special hooks inside the bill allow them to hold onto one fish while catching another. They nest in burrows on grassy cliff-tops. They either dig them out themselves or use old rabbit burrows. They lay one egg and the young bird stays in the burrow until it is six weeks old and fully grown.

Family Group: Auk – Size: Up to 30 cm
Call: Growling 'arr' but silent at sea
Spends winter at sea

Razorbill

Razorbills are generally blacker then Guillemots, but the best way to tell them apart is by the shape of their bills. The Razorbill has a deep black bill with white marks on it. Both Razorbills and Guillemots have short wings, but fly fast. They beat their wings rapidly as they fly. Razorbills also feed on fish. They lay their single eggs among boulders, in rock crevices or down burrows where they have some protection from gulls.

Family Group: Auk
Size: Up to 41 cm
Call: Growls
Spends winter at sea

Guillemot

Family Group: Auk
Size: Up to 42 cm
Call: Silent at sea, noisy in nesting colony
Spends winter at sea

Guillemots look rather like penguins as they stand upright with webbed feet and white underparts. Their backs and wings are dark brown or blackish. Look for the black, pointed bills. They dive underwater for fish, using their short wings as paddles to help them swim. They nest in large, noisy colonies on the steepest cliffs. They build no nest but male and female take it in turn to hold the single egg between their feet. The egg is pear-shaped and spins if it is knocked which makes it less likely to roll off the narrow cliff ledges. When the young are only half-grown they fly out to sea, out of the way of attacking gulls.

Cormorant

You cannot miss these large, black birds. Look for them on rocks and breakwaters, standing with their wings stretched out. Notice the white patch on their face and their long, slightly hooked bill. Watch them dive from the surface of fairly shallow water to hunt for fish. They may stay underwater for up to a minute. Cormorants nest together in colonies. At the coast, they build their nests of seaweed and twigs on a cliff ledge. Inland, they nest in trees. Each female lays three to four eggs.

Family Group: Cormorant
Size: Up to 90 cm
Call: Silent at sea, but honks on nest
Also seen on lakes and rivers

Gannet

Gannets are large white birds with black wing-tips. They are much larger than any gull, their wings measuring almost two metres across. They spend the winter at sea and come to particular parts of the coast to breed in spring and summer. Watch them glide close to the waves or wheel in flocks with other gannets. They feed on fish and dive for them from spectacular heights and at great speed into the sea. They nest in colonies on the ground or on cliff ledges. Breeding females lay just one egg in a nest of seaweed.

Family Group: Gannet
Size: Up to 90 cm
Call: Silent at sea, but croaks in nesting colonies

Shag

Shags are smaller than Cormorants but look very similar, although they have no white on their faces. Their glossy, dark green feathers look black from a distance. In spring and summer, look for the crest on top of the male's head. Shags hunt for fish in deeper water than Cormorants and, like them, they dive from a swimming position. They nest in colonies on cliffs or rocky islets. They lay three or four eggs in a nest of twigs and seaweed.

Family Group: Cormorant
Size: Up to 76 cm – Call: Silent, although croaks and hisses if threatened

Herring Gull

Herring Gulls are larger than Common Gulls and look much fiercer. They are very aggressive birds. Notice the red spot on their yellow bills and pink legs. When the young are hungry, they peck at the red spot, prompting the parents to feed them. Herring Gulls feed on all kinds of food, including other birds' eggs, small mammals and scraps from fishing boats and rubbish tips. They drop shellfish onto rocks to smash the shells. They nest on the ground or on cliff-ledges, but also on roof-tops. They lay three eggs in a nest of grass and other plant material.

Family Group: Gull
Size: Up to 60 cm
Call: 'KEE-YOW'
Also seen inland

Common Gull

Like the Black-headed Gull, you are as likely to see this bird inland as you are at the coast. Its back and wings are grey and its legs are yellowish-green. If it is flying, look for the white spots on its black wing-tips. Common Gulls eat a variety of food, including dead animals, worms, eggs and fish. They sometimes nest among colonies of Herring Gulls at the coast, but most nest on inland lakes and marshes, some singly but others in small groups. They may build a nest of plants or just lay their two or three eggs in a scrape on the ground.

Family Group: Gull – Size: Up to 41 cm
Call: Shrill 'KEE-YA'
Also seen inland

Black-headed Gull

It is easy to identify this gull in summer from its dark brown head, which looks black from a distance. In winter, its head is white, but look for the dark smudge behind each eye and the red beak and legs. You are just as likely to see it in town parks, on refuse tips or following a plough in a field, as at the coast. Black-headed Gulls eat a variety of food, including fish, worms, insects and seeds. They nest on the ground, sometimes in huge colonies of thousands of birds. They lay three eggs in a nest made of bits of plants.

Family Group: Gull
Size: Up to 36 cm
Call: Harsh 'KRAAH'
Also seen inland

Little Gull

These are the smallest gulls of all. They feed by picking food from the water while in flight and also catch insects. Their legs are red and their roundish wings are blackish underneath, but pale grey with a white border on top. In summer, their breasts turn a pinkish colour. The black on their heads shrinks into a grey cap during the winter. The bill is dark red in summer and black in winter. Little Gulls nest in freshwater marshes and swamps, often near lakes. They winter around the coasts of Europe.

Family Group: Gull
Size: Up to 28 cm
Call: Usually silent
Also seen inland

Arctic Tern

Arctic Terns are the world's greatest migrants. They breed in the Arctic and as far south as Scotland, and then fly to the Antarctic for the northern winter. They see more daylight than any other creature! Arctic Terns look just like Common Terns except that their bills are deeper red and do not have a black tip. Like Common Terns, they hover over the sea before diving for fish just below the surface. They nest in colonies with Common Terns and lay one to three eggs in a scrape on the ground or sand. Be careful! They will dive down and peck any intruder who gets too close to their nest.

Family Group: Tern – Size: Up to 35 cm
Call: Higher and harsher than Common Tern's
Summer visitor

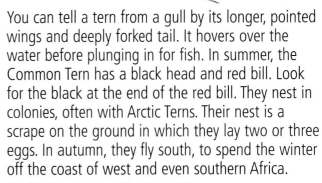

Common Tern

You can tell a tern from a gull by its longer, pointed wings and deeply forked tail. It hovers over the water before plunging in for fish. In summer, the Common Tern has a black head and red bill. Look for the black at the end of the red bill. They nest in colonies, often with Arctic Terns. Their nest is a scrape on the ground in which they lay two or three eggs. In autumn, they fly south, to spend the winter off the coast of west and even southern Africa.

Family Group: Tern – Size: Up to 35 cm
Call: Grating 'KIK-KIK-KIK' – Summer visitor, also seen inland

Kittiwake

Kittiwakes look similar to Common Gulls, but you will hardly ever see them inland. They feed on small fish and shellfish. Their legs are black and their black wing-tips contain no white. If you see a gull with a black 'W' across its wings, it is a young Kittiwake. Kittiwakes nest in colonies. They build large nests of seaweed and mud on cliff ledges and buildings, and lay two or three eggs. The young birds leave the nest and fly out to sea in autumn. They stay there for one or two years before returning to breed.

Family Group: Gull
Size: Up to 41 cm
Call: 'KITTI-WAKE'
Spends winter
at sea

Great Black-backed Gull

This large, fierce gull is easy to recognize from its black back and wings. It has a big head and bill. It preys on Puffins and other seabirds. It also feeds on fish, other birds' eggs, rabbits and shellfish. Great Black-backed Gulls nest on their own or in colonies, on cliffs or high rocks. They lay three eggs in a large nest made from plants.

Family Group: Gull
Size: Up to 70 cm – Call: 'KYOW'

Find Out Some More

Useful organizations

The best organization for you to get in touch with is your local County Wildlife Trust. There are forty-seven of these trusts in Great Britain and you should contact them if you want to know about wildlife and nature reserves and activities in your area. Ask your local library for their address, or contact:

The Wildlife Trusts , The Kiln, Waterside, Mather Road, Newark, Nottinghamshire NG24 1WT (0870 036 7711).

Wildlife Watch is the junior branch of The Wildlife Trusts. Local Wildlife Watch groups run meetings all over the country. Again you can find out about your nearest Wildlife Watch group by contacting The Wildlife Trusts.

The Royal Society for the Protection of Birds (RSPB), The Lodge, Sandy, Beds SG19 2DL (01767 680551) runs many bird sanctuaries in Great Britain and campaigns for the interests of birds.

Wildlife Explorers is the junior branch of the RSPB. By joining you can share your interest in wildlife with like-minded friends. Check out their magazines: *Wild Times* (for the under 8s), *Birdlife* (8-12 years) and *Wingbeat* – written by teenagers for teenagers.

National Trust for Places of Historic Interest or Natural Beauty, 32 Queen Anne's Gate, London SW1H 9AB (01793 817400). For membership and enquiries: The National Trust, PO Box 39, Warrington WA5 7WD (0870 458 4000). They own more than 232,000 hectares of countryside throughout England, Wales and Northern Ireland. These include many woods, nature reserves and sites of special scientific interest. Most are open to visitors, but you usually have to pay to get in. The National Trust also run courses with school groups; ask your teacher to find out about these.

In Scotland, contact the Head of Education **The National Trust for Scotland**, Wemyss House, 28 Charlotte Square, Edinburgh EH2 4ET (0131 243 9300).

The British Trust for Conservation Volunteers (BTCV), Sedum House, Mallard Way, Potteric Carr, Doncaster DN4 8DB (01302 388 888). They work in partnership with landowner, local communities, councils, businesses and charities to protect and maintain rare habitats, footpaths and nature trails. They publish a quarterly magazine, called *The Conserver*, which keeps members up to date with the latest news. They also have a School Membership Scheme; ask your teacher to find out about this.

Places to visit

Birds are everywhere you go from the middle of a big city to the depths of the countryside. Even in a suburban garden, you will be surprised at how many different species will come to your bird table.

However, to see more unusual birds, you will probably have to visit a sanctuary. Ask at your local library or tourist authority.

The RSPB's guide to Nature Reserves (see left) will tell you where to find most of the bird reserves in Britain.

To see the ducks, geese and swans that visit us during the winter, go to the Wildfowl and Wetlands Trust reserves at Slimbridge, in Gloucestershire, at Welney in Cambridgeshire, or at Martin Mere in Lancashire. Other exciting places include the Solway Firth and the East Anglian coast.

For more exotic birds, go to your local zoo or wildlife park. Often these have regular displays by birds of prey, and afterwards you can look at the birds close to and talk to their handlers.

Index & Glossary

To find the name of a bird in this index, search under its family name. So, to look up Marsh Harrier, look under Harrier, not under Marsh.

Index & Glossary